The Intelligent Heart

D1208288

ALSO BY DZIGAR KONGTRUL

It's Up to You: The Practice of
Self-Reflection on the Buddhist Path

Light Comes Through: Buddhist Teachings on
Awakening to Our Natural Intelligence

Uncommon Happiness: The Path of
the Compassionate Warrior

The Intelligent Heart

A Guide to the Compassionate Life

Dzigar Kongtrul

Foreword by Pema Chödrön

SHAMBHALA · BOULDER · 2016

Shambhala Publications, Inc.
4720 Walnut Street
Boulder, Colorado 80301
www.shambhala.com

© 2016 by Dzigar Kongtrul
All rights reserved. No part of this book may be reproduced in
any form or by any means, electronic or mechanical, including
photocopying, recording, or by any information storage and retrieval
system, without permission in writing from the publisher.

9 8 7 6 5 4 3 2 1

First Edition
Printed in the United States of America

♾ This edition is printed on acid-free paper that meets the
American National Standards Institute z39.48 Standard.
♻ This book is printed on 30% postconsumer recycled paper.
For more information please visit www.shambhala.com.

Distributed in the United States by Penguin Random House LLC
and in Canada by Random House of Canada Ltd

Designed by Lance Hidy

LIBRARY OF CONGRESS CATALOGING-IN-PUBLICATION DATA
Names: Kongtrul, Dzigar.
Title: The intelligent heart: a guide to the compassionate life /
Dzigar Kongtrul; foreword by Pema Chödrön.
Description: First Edition. | Boulder: Shambhala, 2016.
Identifiers: LCCN 2015026376 | ISBN 9781611801781 (pbk.: alk. paper)
Subjects: LCSH: Compassion—Religious aspects—Buddhism. |
Religious life—Buddhism.
Classification: LCC BQ4360.K66 2016 | DDC 294.3/444—dc23 LC
record available at http://lccn.loc.gov/2015026376

May bodhicitta, precious and sublime,
Arise where it has not yet come to be;
And where it has arisen may it never fail
But grow and flourish ever more and more.

Contents

Foreword

There has never been a time when human beings have been free from confusion and pain, but these days things seem especially tough. You can feel it in the atmosphere. Dealing with the habits that cause ourselves and the world suffering has become a life-and-death matter. People are asking, "What can I do?"

The book you are holding is full of practical solutions. Though the lojong teachings have been around for a thousand years, they are very much teachings for this age. Lojong aims directly at the core of our confused mind and gives us a multitude of tips for working with our habits on the spot. Yet lojong doesn't dwell on our confusion. Its purpose is to uncover the basic wisdom and compassion that is our deepest nature. We practice lojong to connect to the natural tenderness of our heart by opening up instead of closing down. We aim to wake ourselves up so that we can help others do the same.

I feel that there is no better teacher to present this wisdom to a modern audience than Dzigar Kongtrul Rinpoche. I have known Rinpoche since the mid-1990s, when we met at a Buddhist teachers' conference. Since the passing of my root teacher, Chögyam Trungpa Rinpoche, I hadn't met anyone who could sense where I was stuck. I was very good at conning everyone and talking about not getting hooked, but Rinpoche somehow had this great ability to hook me. Soon after our meeting, I asked if he would take me as his student, and he accepted. He's continued to mess with me ever since.

Because the original work is very pithy, it can be quite difficult for a modern audience to appreciate. Rinpoche's commentary makes this classic text come to life. His way of explaining the material is a great inspiration for my own teaching. Rinpoche has a wonderful sense of humor, but he's also very wrathful at times and pushes your nose into some of the undesirable qualities we human beings exhibit. You will see yourself in this book. You may not see yourself in every example, but there is something for everybody.

—PEMA CHÖDRÖN

Acknowledgments

First and foremost I would like to acknowledge and pay my deepest obeisance to my root teacher, His Holiness Dilgo Khyentse Rinpoche, from whom I have received these teachings on *The Mahayana Instructions on the Seven Points of Mind Training,* along with all my other teachers who have greatly helped me to understand the lojong teachings. I would also like to acknowledge my debt of gratitude to Gyalse Ngulchu Tokme and Jamgon Kongtrul Lodro Thaye for their poignant and succinct commentaries on the slogans, in which they expound on their meaning, expertly illuminating particular human experiences of the egotistical mind. Without their commentaries it would have been very difficult to understand precisely what the slogans are addressing within us, as the language is profoundly dense and written in ancient colloquial Tibetan. I also pay homage to the great Mahapandita Dipamkara, who was solely responsible for reviving Mahayana Buddhism in Tibet after its initial influence had declined. And I pay deep reverence to the great and unparalleled string of pearls, the Kadampa Gewé Shényen, in particular, to Chekawa Yeshe Dorje, who put these teachings into the format of the *Seven Points.*

Since first hearing the lojong teachings I took a deep interest in them and became inspired to study them as a synthesis of all Mahayana and Vajrayana teachings. The little bit of understanding of them that I have come to have has greatly reduced my own suffering, though I claim no realization or knowledge whatsoever. Any understanding I have is due to the continuous blessings of my great teachers, starting with my own root lama and many other illustrious beings of this world, and His

Holiness the Fourteenth Dalai Lama, from whom I draw great inspiration foremost among them. They are the true spokesmen of lojong practice. When I hear their profound expositions on lojong, such as the *Seven Points* or the *Bodhicaryavatara,* I begin to feel their blessings plowing the hard soil of my mind, uprooting and exposing countless self-centered attitudes from many lifetimes, turning those into good pliable ground in which to sow the seeds of liberation.

In the collection of the commentaries on the *Seven Points,* there is a text with no known author, but it is most profound and its timeless blessings have greatly benefited me.

I have tried to personally study these teachings and, in order to enhance my own practice and understanding, I have also taught them on several occasions with the aim of familiarizing my own mind and experience with the deeper layers of the lojong. This text is a result of that process, which our Khenchung Joseph Waxman has compiled into this book. I truly appreciate his work here in going through each of these teaching occasions and painstakingly gathering the threads from various angles and approaches in order to give each of the slogans their fullest treatment. I am delighted to see the fruits of his efforts.

I am also very humbled and honored that this book is a commentary on *The Mahayana Instructions on the Seven Points of Mind Training.* I do not consider it to be any sort of great exposition on the lojong from any standard of high realization or scriptural authority. Nonetheless, for modern people in these modern times, I hope it brings some benefit and therefore gives justice to this endeavor.

Please forgive me for any errors, mistakes, or presumptuousness, as though I were someone who understood the lojong teachings from experience. Such a claim would obviously in itself be contrary to the lojong teachings. Nonetheless, whatever benefit this small text brings to modern readers for uprooting the self-centeredness that we all suffer from, and for enhancing the altruism that we all have as our potential, will bring me great joy, and I wholeheartedly dedicate the merit of this to the true benefit of beings.

I would also like to extend my most heartfelt thanks for all the effort and care that took place behind the scenes from so many people, without whom this book could never have evolved. I thank all the audio technicians whose precise and detailed work ensured the talks were captured and archived, especially Paddy McCarthy and the Wisdom Productions team of Mangala Shri Bhuti, who work tirelessly and consistently to track, collect, and archive all the teachings that happen. And to the ranks of dedicated transcribers: I truly appreciate your time and hope that listening to and typing out the transcripts has brought your own minds closer to the lojong teachings. I also want to acknowledge the graduates of Guna Institute and Vairochana's Legacy, Mangala Shri Bhuti's translation team, for collaborating so skillfully in their translation of the *Seven Points* and Jamgon Kongtrul's commentary. I hope that this new translation only enhances the wonderful translations that have already been so expertly accomplished. May your efforts serve to deepen your own understanding of dharma and deepen your personal practice. I would also like to thank those who have offered financial support for the writing of this book through their generous contributions to Mangala Shri Bhuti's Dharma Book Fund.

And most especially I would like to thank Shambhala Publications: Dave O'Neal, the editor of this work; Ben Gleason, the assistant editor; Leda Scheintaub, the copy editor; Emily White, the proofreader; and a very special and heartfelt thanks to both Nikko Odiseos and Jonathan Green, the president and vice president of Shambhala Publications, who have been marvelously supportive throughout this process. I deeply rejoice in Shambhala's efforts to bring the dharma to a modern readership, and I make prayers of dedication that the merit of your work bring great benefit to yourselves and all sentient beings without limit. Your vision and effort have been, are, and will continue to be paramount in the transplantation of the dharma in the West. May Shambhala's activity, especially in this area, continue long into the future.

Editor's Introduction

When Dzigar Kongtrul Rinpoche was teaching in Ireland several years ago, he learned how mussels are cultivated off the Irish coast. The farmers attach mussel seeds to long ropes that hang under water. Clinging to the ropes, the mussels grow until they are large enough to be eaten. Although there is nothing preventing these creatures from letting go and floating away, they remain in place until the ropes are pulled up and they are scraped off and boiled alive. For Rinpoche, this story illustrates the basic misunderstanding that rules our lives, causing every form of unhappiness and suffering that we experience. Just as the mussels hold tightly to their fatal rope, so too do we hold on desperately to our self, this all-important being we call *me*. Hearing about the mussels, Rinpoche said, made him "sad and curious."

Rinpoche has been teaching the dharma for close to thirty years, since he was in his early twenties. He has taught on five continents, to people of every description, from a vast range of source texts. But every single teaching he gives is permeated by the same point. The only way to obtain the peace, joy, and fulfillment that all of us long for is by releasing our tight hold on *me* and turning our attention to the welfare of others.

These complementary aims can be achieved through the transformative practice of *tonglen,* also known as the exchange of self and other. Tonglen is the subject of this book. Though tonglen is extremely simple as an idea, the human mind is expert at complicating things. Because the exchange of self and other goes against the grain of our habitual self-centeredness, we put up many levels of resistance, from gross to subtle. Thus there is a lot to say about this subject.

Though Rinpoche is renowned for his ability to reach modern audiences and get to the essence of our particular brands of confusion, he has often found it beneficial to base his teachings on those of the great masters of the past. These traditional works show the timelessness and universality of Buddhist wisdom. They are also permeated by the blessings of all the subsequent generations that they have transformed. One of the teachings Rinpoche holds closest to his heart is *The Mahayana Instructions on the Seven Points of Mind Training* by the twelfth-century Tibetan teacher Chekawa Yeshe Dorje. This work broadly falls into the category of *lojong* (mind transformation) teachings, the essence of which is tonglen. Rinpoche has given volumes of oral commentary on the *Seven Points*. The book you are holding is distilled from more than one hundred hours of teachings Rinpoche gave between 2001 and 2015 in Australia, Ireland, France, Taiwan, and various parts of the United States.

This book came about as the result of two of Rinpoche's inspirations. The first is his passion for tonglen and the *Seven Points,* and his conviction in their ability to transform people in the modern age. Second, this book includes a new translation of one of the most important commentaries of the *Seven Points, The Seven Points of Mahayana Mind Training: A Guide to Benefit Those Embarking on the Authentic Path to Enlightenment,* by Jamgon Kongtrul Lodro Thaye. From 2007 to 2012, Rinpoche led a program in northern India in which he taught twelve students how to translate the dharma from Tibetan into English. His Eminence Tai Situ Rinpoche named this group Vairochana's Legacy, in honor of one of the greatest translators of Sanskrit to Tibetan. This rendering is the first fruition of their efforts. While it is not intended to supersede previous translations of Jamgon Kongtrul's commentary (such as the excellent version by Ken McLeod titled *The Great Path of Awakening*), we hope that it will further illuminate what is already available, and that it will be a joy to read.

—JOSEPH WAXMAN

The Intelligent Heart

Introduction

It All Started with Tonglen

It is said that the Buddha began his path to enlightenment one thousand lifetimes before he took birth as an Indian prince. He and his friend were suffering the torments of a hellish existence. They were forced to pull an impossibly heavy cart up a steep hill by straps tied to their foreheads. The cart would hardly budge, but every time they tried to rest, their ruthless guard would whip them. At one point, the future Buddha, despite his unbearable pain, saw how much his friend was suffering and felt an unexpected surge of compassion. He asked the guard if he could take the entire load himself so that his friend could rest. The angry guard replied, "You can't prevent someone from experiencing the result of his actions!" With that he struck the Buddha in the head, knocking him out.

When the Buddha came to, he was in a completely different realm, a place where he had the opportunity and peace of mind to continue deepening the altruistic impulse that had first entered his mind in hell. He was now on the path to letting go of his own self-interest and putting the interest of others first. He was now on the path to becoming the fully enlightened Buddha, who appeared in our world 2,500 years ago and has had a profoundly beneficial effect on humankind ever since.

In the story of the Buddha, this is the first example of the power of *tonglen*. The Tibetan word *tong* means "giving"; *len* means "taking." In its most well-known form, tonglen is a meditation technique that involves coordination with the breath. Breathing in, we visualize ourselves *taking* on the suffering of others; breathing out, we visualize ourselves *giving* others happiness. This powerful method for transforming our minds vividly illustrates the exchange of self and other that is the essence and spirit of tonglen. But the wider meaning and application of tonglen, both in spiritual practice and ordinary life, goes far beyond this specific technique. In general, *tonglen* refers to any form of exchanging self and other. We can even apply the term to the mundane exchange between an employer who pays wages and an employee who does work. Since, as we will see, the entire aim of the Buddhist path is to lessen the importance of the self and to increase the importance of others, tonglen is at the very heart of all practices. Without having an orientation toward tonglen, it is unlikely that our spiritual path will have a profound effect on our mind and heart.

But before I go into too much detail about techniques for contemplation and meditation, I want to start off by saying more about what the teachings mean by these crucial terms, *self* and *other*. Without precisely understanding what these words mean—in the books, but more important, in our own experience—it will be easy to go astray and mistake tonglen for other things, such as being a martyr or beating up on ourselves. It's important to see, right off the bat, that practicing tonglen is in our best interest, leading toward the freedom, peace, and joy we all seek in our lives.

First, I'll begin with *self,* which sometimes goes by the name *ego,* or more familiarly, *I* and *me*. What is this self, really? We can investigate by trying to analyze this self, to locate it or pin it down, to see if it even exists in the first place. This can be a highly illuminating contemplation, but for the purposes of this book, I would like to focus more on our everyday experience. Let's identify how having a self feels. In our mind stream, there is always some kind of feeling of having a self, which is at the center of all our thoughts and emotions. One Tibetan phrase targets this phenomenon precisely: *dak che dzin*. *Dak* means "self"; *che* means "important" or "dear"; *dzin* means "holding" or "regarding." This term has various translations, which all capture different nuances:

self-centeredness, self-clinging, ego-clinging, self-absorption. I like to use all of these terms in different contexts, but my favorite translation is "self-importance." This word may make us think *dak che dzin* has mostly to do with being proud and arrogant, but such pride is nowhere near the whole story. Self-importance includes both self-cherishing and self-protection. It is the source of the five main types of painful emotions, known as the "five poisons": attachment, aggression, jealousy, arrogance, and stupidity. It can manifest as feeling like we're better than others, but just as easily it can manifest as low self-esteem, or even self-hatred. The bottom line is that we regard this self—whatever or wherever it is—as the most important thing in the entire universe.

Self-importance can be blatant or extremely subtle. In fact, most of the time, it's not obvious to us. It doesn't just pop out and announce itself. And even if we can see it clearly, we don't usually find anything wrong with it. Either we don't have the knowledge that self-importance is a problem, or we simply don't want to see it as a problem. But according to the Buddhist teachings—and we will explore this idea further in the course of this book—all the suffering we have ever experienced, all that we experience now, and all that we will experience in the future, come from self-importance.

Anyone who has been studying Buddhism for some time has probably heard this notion expressed many times. But what is our reaction to this statement? Do we take it seriously, or do we say "Yeah, yeah…"? Are we even open to the possibility of accepting this idea? Our tendency is to pick and choose what we would *like* to be the cause of our suffering. The cause we choose is almost always something outside ourselves. Basically, the world and the people in it are failing in their duty to make us happy. We can manipulate the world and even try to demand that it bring us fulfillment, but the world will always refuse to play along. In fact, having this attitude is precisely what prevents us from having peace and joy in our lives. Shantideva, the author of *The Way of the Bodhisattva,* perhaps the greatest work on this subject, hits the nail on the head with this famous and provocative statement:

"All the misery the world contains has come from wanting pleasure for oneself."

If we look around, the evidence for these words is ample. There is a visible difference in well-being between people who focus on helping others and people who are preoccupied with their own pleasure. Yet there is still something inside us that refuses to acknowledge the evidence. What is that something? It is none other than our self-importance. This puts us in a tricky situation. The thing that chooses—incorrectly—what to blame for our suffering is the very same thing that causes all our suffering. We tend to give our self-importance absolute and unquestioned authority over our lives. We are so enmeshed with it that we have no idea how we could ever let it go. The thought of letting it go can bring on such a mental disturbance that it almost feels like letting go of a baby that we're holding over the edge of a cliff. Letting go of our self-importance can feel like insanity.

Can you recognize this feeling within yourself? Can you feel it viscerally? Can you find it in your body, speech, and mind, in your thoughts, emotions, and actions? If so, then you know what I mean by *dak che dzin,* self-importance. If you don't feel it, then ask yourself a few simple questions: At this moment, what is guiding your mental and emotional state? What is guiding your body, speech, and mind? Is it altruism? If it's not altruism, what is it?

Our self-importance usually doesn't display itself in an obnoxious Hollywood way. I once saw a movie in which a character declared: "I'm brilliant! No, really! Monuments should be erected in my honor!" If our self-importance goes that far, we may notice it. But in general, we take it for granted that self-importance is our guiding principle. And even when we do have an inkling of its existence, it is rare for us to slow down and penetrate it.

If we want to have any chance of resisting this troublesome authority of our lives, we have to take the time to sit down and feel it. In order to do so, however, we need to do our best to look at it without judgment. If our examination of self-importance turns into self-disparagement or beating up on ourselves, then how likely are we to keep going with this crucial, life-changing process? How much will we want to investigate what's going on, if the result will only be to find out how terrible we are?

Therefore, the most helpful attitude to have is to see yourself as innocent. Identify with that innocence rather than with the self-importance. You are innocent, but within your heart there is a spoiled rotten rascal who is totally out of control. This rascal is always causing you pain, so many forms of pain. You can't predict the next problem it will make you face. Because of this rascal and its demands, you always have to be on your toes, anxious, struggling, tense. It bosses you around, making you work yourself to exhaustion, like a slave driver. If you don't obey it and meet its needs, it will throw a tantrum. This may all sound like exaggeration, but when we sit with our self-importance long enough and get to know it well, we can recognize it for the rascal it is.

When you recognize it, you may at first feel stuck. What can you do about such a powerful, all-pervasive slave driver who has made a cozy home in your heart? You may feel doomed to permanent enslavement, but in reality you have taken the first step to starting a revolution inside yourself. Before starting a revolution, you must first have a resistance movement. And for that, you need concrete, intelligent reasons for resisting. It won't help your resistance to rely on unclear, emotional, abstract reasoning. When the reasons for a resistance or a revolution are not clear and precise, the movement can be easily infiltrated and bought by the enemy, as has happened many times in human history. Similarly, when we are not clear about how self-importance harms ourselves and others, and about the benefits of counteracting it, our Buddhist practices can actually increase our self-importance. When that happens we truly do become stuck. Then we may be in serious trouble.

So that is why it is crucial to take the time to identify self-importance at the outset. Once we do so, we will come to realize that we have an innate intelligence capable of overthrowing the rascal. For in reality, our self-importance, despite the havoc it causes, is severely limited. Since it always looks outward and never self-reflects, it is quite stupid. Actually, it is more than just stupid; I would go so far as to call it the epitome of stupidity. That is why we can have hope in banishing the rascal from our heart, and with it all of our suffering.

Now that we have some idea of "self" and the problems that come from making it so important, we can turn our attention to identifying the other side of the coin. That is *zhen che dzin,* which means "holding others as important and dear." A simple translation that captures most of the meaning is "altruism." It seems easy to identify this feeling when it comes to your family and friends. You cherish them because you have a bond with them. But what is the basis of that bond? The basis is that these select individuals are related to *you.* They're *yours.* In other words, your self-importance is again involved. Occasionally you may see a bug drowning in a pool of water and feel enough compassion to rescue it. In that case, cherishing the "other" is more clean and fresh since it lacks the scent of self-importance. But such cases are relatively rare in our lives.

This doesn't mean, however, that you can only understand the value of caring for others if that care is completely untainted. Even with the scent of self-importance, to feel love for your children or parents feels great. Without having people or animals to love, your existence would be dull and miserable. Your love for others is what keeps you going. It gives you energy, brightness, and a sense of purpose. But the highest love, the love we aspire to on the Buddhist path, is without a trace of self-importance. This is the love of the bodhisattvas, those who strive to develop their wisdom and compassion to the highest possible level in order to lead all beings to ultimate and permanent happiness. This bodhisattva love is really what we are setting out to develop when we practice tonglen.

In the beginning it may seem that such a love is impossible. At the very least it seems unnatural. Are we supposed to conjure something up that our heart doesn't naturally produce? It's natural to love your own child, but to love someone else's child equally takes a lot of work. We are comfortable confining our deep love to a few people close to us, but if we would like to grow as individuals and eventually become bodhisattvas, we have to go beyond these limits.

Fortunately, there is a straightforward and gradual method for doing this. We start with the love we already have, acknowledging its power and the great joy it gives us. And then we spread that love toward all other beings. This sounds simple enough, but how do we actually spread our love? We begin by looking within. If at this very moment you look at what is going on in your thoughts and emotions, you will notice something very basic and obvious. In your mind you are constantly trying to move toward happiness and away from suffering. Every little thing that appears to your five senses or that arises in your thoughts falls into one of three categories. You like it, you dislike it, or you don't really notice it. Your mind is continually reacting in these ways: grasping, rejecting, ignoring. You never get a break from this process, even while dreaming. Look at your mind and see if this is true.

Once you've seen your own mind in this way, the next step is to put yourself in the shoes of another living being. It could be anyone you think of, from the president of the United States to an ant. The president seems all-important, and the ant seems insignificant, but from their point of view, is their essential moment-to-moment experience any different from yours? The president may be pondering whether to bomb a foreign country, while the ant is merely transporting a bread crumb, but both continually experience the basic grasping and rejection, the never-ending desire and fear that underlies the experience of all beings.

When we spend time thinking along these lines, we inevitably will conclude that we and all other living beings are equal in our desire for happiness. We and all other beings are equal in our longing to be free from suffering. Once we acknowledge this to be true, it becomes much harder to separate ourselves and our loved ones from the limitless numbers of sentient beings in the universe. What would we accomplish by focusing on such an extremely tiny group? And what would we have to lose by expanding our care to all beings? Say you are in a refugee camp and find yourself in the position of being able to help every refugee there get to a safer, more stable place. You have this chance, but instead you just run away with your immediate family. Wouldn't that be small-minded? Wouldn't you be failing to meet your potential?

Ultimately, our true potential is to live like a bodhisattva. Bodhisattvas do not hold back by thinking they can only do so much for others. Because they deeply contemplate how all beings equally desire happiness and freedom from pain, bodhisattvas develop a bond with everyone. Therefore they never shy away from manifesting their full potential. The more our orientation shifts toward the well-being of others—and away from catering to the persistent but stupid rascal in our heart—the more we will experience the deep peace and joy of the Buddha's wisdom. For, as Shantideva said in *The Way of the Bodhisattva,* in counterpoint to the previous quote: "All the joy the world contains comes from wishing happiness for others."

To present the rich subject of tonglen in all its depth and variety, I have chosen to write about it in the context of the well-known Tibetan teaching *The Mahayana Instructions on the Seven Points of Mind Training (theg pa chenpo'i gdams ngag blo sbyong don bdun ma bzhugs so)* by Chekawa Yeshe Dorje. This work belongs to the class of teachings called *lojong*. We all have a mind (*lo*), and this mind is always undergoing training (*jong*). Once we have been exposed to these teachings, we have a choice: to make an effort to train our mind in a productive way, or to let our mind train itself. If we choose the second, default, option, our only guide will be our mind's constant and malicious adviser, self-importance. Instead of getting out of the rut it has always been in, our mind will continue to develop and perpetuate habits based on the whims of a rascal. Despite our constant efforts to achieve happiness and freedom from suffering, we will create more and more of the opposite results in our lives. So rather than subjecting our mind to endless torment, we can employ the methods of lojong, which have transformed the minds of innumerable people through the ages.

In the eighth century, Buddhism enjoyed its greatest period of blossoming in Tibet. King Trisong Detsen, whose mission in life was to fully transplant the dharma from the Noble Land of India to Tibet, invited the great scholar Shantarakshita and the incomparably powerful Guru Padmasambhava to establish the teachings, practices, traditions, and physical structures in his kingdom. This period saw the founding of the first Tibetan monastery, the ordaining of the first Tibetan monks, the translation of countless texts into Tibetan, and the establishment of the first lineages of fully enlightened Tibetan practitioners. Within a short time, the entire range of Buddhist teachings and practices had been firmly transplanted into this formerly wild country.

Eventually, however, the dharma in Tibet became weak and diluted. Practitioners had lost sight of the point of dharma and were using it more and more to fortify their self-importance. So in the eleventh century, King Lha Lama Yeshe O, saddened by the dharma's decline, looked to India again for another master who could restore its purity. He chose to invite Atisha Dipamkara, at that time the best-known teacher in India. Although Atisha was a master of all the classical texts and every form of Buddhist practice, he emphasized the themes of lojong and tonglen: letting go of self-importance and developing altruism. To help his students train their minds in this positive direction, he used pithy slogans, which were easy to understand and memorize. With these methods, Atisha was able to shine a light on all that was going on in Tibetan culture, and to make it clear what was true dharma and what was not. For a long time after Atisha's period, Buddhism in Tibet was very pure.

Atisha passed on his lineage to his close disciples, and a few generations later, Chekawa Yeshe Dorje (1102–76) wrote down these teachings, which were later organized as the *The Mahayana Instructions on the Seven Points of Mind Training*, fifty-nine slogans divided into seven categories. This presentation of lojong, which makes up the framework of this book, has remained popular to this very day and has been the basis of commentaries by many of the greatest minds in Tibet. Since I do not consider myself to be in the same class as any of these illustrious teachers, I have based my own teachings on one of the most renowned commentaries, *The Seven Points of Mahayana Mind Training: A Guide to Benefit Those Embarking on the Authentic Path to Enlightenment* (*theg pa chenpo blo sbyong don bdun ma'i khrid yig blo dman 'jug bder bkod pa byang chub gzhung lam zhes bay ba zhugs so*). This text was written in the nineteenth century by Jamgon Kongtrul Lodro Thaye, who devoted most of his life to preserving the eight lineages of Tibetan Buddhism by collecting teachings and practices, learning the essence of each tradition, and writing many volumes of commentaries based on his deep understanding. Since I have been recognized by my own teacher as one of Jamgon Kongtrul's reincarnations, I feel a special connection to his explanations and will do my best to illuminate them for a modern audience.

Point One

The Preliminaries Teach the Foundation of Dharma Practice

1. First, train in the preliminaries.

In our day-to-day life, our mind tends to follow a certain exhausting track. We are constantly engaged in thoughts, which shape our feelings and attitudes. These thoughts are usually based on sensory perceptions. We see or hear something and think that it's beautiful or ugly, pleasant or unpleasant. If it's pleasant, we mentally grasp after it; if it's unpleasant, we mentally reject it. If neither, our mental state becomes dull in relation to the object. When we wander off into the past, we occupy ourselves with memories of pleasantness and unpleasantness, and we continue to grasp and reject. Our plans and visions for the future also involve a lot of ideas of what will be pleasant and unpleasant. This is how our thought process operates, all day long, in subtle and gross forms. Going through a day like this, with such a reactive mind, is emotionally exhausting. Then we go to sleep and withdraw into dreams, and sometimes even further into a blank state of mind. We are trying to restore ourselves and gain fresh mental and physical energy to wake up and engage with the world for the next round. This is the self-centered rut in which our mind tends to operate. This is how our life generally goes along.

"First, train in the preliminaries" encourages us to make time in our lives to shape our mind intentionally, rather than staying in this rut. Taking some time every day, even as little as five minutes, for some contemplation will help us to use our mind to its best capacity and to develop clarity and perspective about our lives. Jamgon Kongtrul organizes this preliminary contemplation into four parts: (1) the difficulty of attaining the freedoms and endowments, (2) death and impermanence, (3) the defects of samsara, and (4) contemplating the cause and result of karma.

Contemplating "the difficulty of attaining the freedoms and endowments" means contemplating the preciousness of our life, the very situation we have right now. All sentient beings feel their lives are precious, but here we are talking about something more. We have the rare and incredible fortune to have the dharma in our lives. More specifically, we have teachings that lead us away from our habitual self-importance and in the direction of a much more beneficial and fulfilling altruism.

Imagine that you find yourself in the middle of the Sahara Desert, in an infinite vastness of sand. You can't just hang out there. The sun is too hot and there is no food or water. You have no idea which way to go. You have no reference point: in every direction all you can see is sand and more sand. Nevertheless you feel compelled to walk. What else can you do? But the more you walk, the more sand you see. There's no sign of anything but desert—and therefore no hope of any positive outcome. Eventually you will just drop dead, having accomplished nothing.

Now imagine that you miraculously discover a map, which shows you exactly where you are, why you have been going around aimlessly, and in which direction you need to travel. You find that food, water, and shelter are not hopelessly far away. You have a clear path to survival. Revived by this discovery, you set out in the right direction and become free from your awful predicament.

In our analogy, the Sahara represents our habitual self-importance, which is so all-encompassing that it seems to have no beginning and no end. The map, which leads us in the direction of altruism, represents *bodhicitta,* a Sanskrit word that can be translated as "the mind-set of awakening." Bodhicitta is the state of mind of the bodhisattvas, those who strive to attain enlightenment for the sake of all sentient beings, devoting themselves, without limit or hesitation, to fulfilling this aim.

As we will see throughout this book, this extraordinary mind-set is really what we are aiming to develop when we do lojong practices such as tonglen. We all long to be happy and free from suffering, but without bodhicitta we have no orientation toward that happiness and freedom. The attitude of bodhicitta, and the practices that help promote it, give us a way of dealing with our present suffering, and of eventually transcending suffering altogether.

How bodhicitta works is very simple. When we look outward and see how much all other beings are suffering—even though they want to be happy just as much as we do—then our care for our small, individual self naturally transforms into care for a much bigger "self." We grow from having self-care to universal care. Right away our own suffering becomes smaller. It doesn't instantly and totally disappear, but diminishes naturally and progressively as we free ourselves from attachment to the small self. When the sun shines, it absorbs all the light of the moon and stars into its brightness. Similarly, when we have bodhicitta, the brilliant light of our universal love and care outshines and absorbs our concerns for this one individual.

Instead of dropping dead in the Sahara from thirst, we can travel purposefully and confidently along the bodhisattva's path, until we reach its culmination, which is the complete and irreversible awakening to our own true nature: in a word, "enlightenment." Since our true nature is identical to that of the Buddha, when we awaken to it we will be free from all illusions and enjoy limitless wisdom, love, and power to benefit others. Having the opportunity to start to realize our potential in such a magnificent way is why our life is so precious.

Once we've inspired ourselves by thinking about our precious opportunity, we should move on to the second preliminary contemplation: death and impermanence. If we want to make the best of our life by developing our bodhicitta, we can't keep putting it off. We will not be in this world much longer. Even if you're very young and have as many as eighty more years still to live, eighty years isn't much. When I taught at Naropa University, I had a good friend who was quite sharp at the age of ninety-two. She used to come to all my classes and be very active. Before she died, I asked her if it seemed like she'd had a long life or if it had gone by quickly. She said it went by like a flash of lightning. When we look back from our deathbed, that is what we'll see. In our youth, time seemed to pass more slowly, but from this point on, it will go faster and faster—and then it will be over. And there is no guarantee we will make it to old age. There is no guarantee we'll live even one more year, or one more month. There are no grounds even to assume we won't die in our sleep tonight. How could there be? Our life is like a butter lamp in the wind or a bubble in a stream. It is completely unstable.

We can think about great beings from the past: kings and queens and other grand figures who were so important and full of life. Now they are all gone. There is no one here from the century before last, let alone those distant ages. Even the enlightened ones from the past, who achieved mastery over the physical elements and were able to perform miracles, have gone from this world. In our own families, if we go back just a few generations, nobody is still alive. Most of us don't even know the names of our great-grandparents. And many of the people we've known in this life are no longer here. Even the memories of their faces are fading from our minds. This will also happen to ourselves. Soon I will be gone. So will you.

So while we are here for this short time, what is the point of doing anything but dedicating ourselves to bodhicitta, to tonglen, to stepping out of the small self and embracing the universal self? Some of our daily activities are necessary to sustain us, but trying to secure ourselves as if we're going to live forever is foolish. No one has ever been able to secure anything. Why would we be different? Look at how the four seasons change. Can we secure one season and prevent it from transitioning to the next? "I like summer. I'm going to hold on to it and not face autumn and winter." We can have these thoughts, but autumn and winter will still come, followed by spring, and then we'll see another summer—if we're still around. This may all be obvious, but in order for it to sink in to our minds and hearts deeply, we have to take the time to contemplate. Otherwise we'll continue to act in ways that don't really make sense.

Contemplating impermanence helps us have a simpler approach to life, in which we no longer create kingdoms in our minds. If you are reading this book, you most likely have the basic necessities of life: food, clothing, shelter. Trying to get more than that and put everything in its perfect place comes from buying into delusions that are based on a sense of permanence. But if we think from the point of view of a person about to exit from this world, we can save ourselves a lot of trouble, a lot of energy, and a lot of money. All our attachments, our efforts, our stress, our anxiety—are they really worth it? Do we need to keep up with all our activities and attachments and every e-mail that comes into our inbox, or should we simplify? If we want to enjoy our life, does it help to be a workaholic, a worry-holic, an attached-holic? Isn't that like desperately trying to rearrange your furniture while your house is burning down?

When we die, we won't be able to take anything with us, not even our own body. As they say in Tibet, our mind will travel alone from this life to the next, like a hair pulled from butter. The butter in Tibet often has yak hairs in it. But when you pull one out, it is completely clean, without a trace of butter. Recognizing that our mind will travel so nakedly keeps us from becoming enslaved by attachment. Our life becomes much simpler, and as a result our mind becomes more calm and clear. In this state, we can finally start enjoying life. And we can have the space to develop our bodhicitta, which will lead to greater and greater happiness, both for ourselves and for an ever-widening circle of living beings we're connected to. By studying teachings such as the *Seven Points,* we can develop the knack of turning any situation in life into a chance to practice. Once we have understood and absorbed these simple and accessible teachings, we will never lack opportunities to cultivate bodhicitta. If we take advantage of these opportunities, we will have no regrets at the end of our life.

After contemplating death and impermanence, it's then helpful to think about things from another point of view. What will happen if we ignore our opportunity and carry on as we always have, by clinging to this small self as if it's the only thing in the universe that matters? To answer that question, we must examine our own mind and how it habitually suffers. This is the third subject to contemplate when training in the preliminaries, "the defects of samsara." The Sanskrit word *samsara* refers to the perpetual cycle of suffering that we sentient beings go through as a result of our innocent but ignorant self-importance. This cycle will never come to an end unless the rascal in our heart is recognized for what it is and banished forever.

We human beings are very resilient. However much we suffer, when the pain is over we tend to move on and forget. In a way, that is admirable. But if there's something we can actually do about our suffering, if we can eliminate its causes and thus become free, if peace and happiness are realistic possibilities, then does it make sense just to keep suffering? When we have some understanding of the causes of suffering but insist on bearing it over and over again, never learning our lesson, would you say that such resilience is intelligent?

The countless ways that we suffer can be put into three categories: physical, emotional, and mental. Physical suffering, unless it's severe or chronic, is the easiest kind to work with. You may have a headache right now, but you aren't so troubled because there's something you can do about it. Because you have some aspirin in the bathroom and know you can take it at any time, you may even be able to ignore your headache for a while and do something else. Knowing what the problem is and how to fix it puts your mind relatively at ease.

We have less tolerance to emotional pain because it's harder to understand. Our emotional world is murkier than our physical world. For example, we may feel vaguely insecure. Without fully realizing what we're doing, we act to cover up that insecurity. When we aren't able to cover it up, we feel emotionally threatened. It's not clear to us what we're trying to do, or how or why we feel threatened, but feeling threatened makes us reactive. We either react outwardly by losing our temper, or inwardly with negative thinking and judgments. We may go through our daily activities, appearing to others as if nothing's going on, but in our emotions we continually suffer. Because this pain is so hard to get a handle on, it's very difficult to work with. If we can't trace it to a cause, how can we apply a remedy? And to make matters worse, we have little or no tolerance for our negative thoughts and emotions. We want so badly to be *good*. Of course it's good to be good, but when we can't live up to our idea of good, we put tremendous pressure on ourselves. This adds to our emotional pain and causes us to react further, bringing about even more suffering. This chain reaction is but one of countless examples that show how vulnerable we are to emotional suffering.

Then we have our mental suffering, the pain of our conceptual mind. This is the suffering of ignorance, which comes in two basic forms. First, we don't know what's going on in our mental process, what is arising moment by moment. We can't see how cause and effect operate in our mind and how we continually create and re-create our own suffering. All we know, and usually only vaguely, is that we want things to be different. The second way we're ignorant is that even if we have a glimpse of what's going on, we have no idea what to do about it. Not knowing what's happening and not knowing what to do are both deeply painful. We may not be aware of this, but we go through life feeling constantly bewildered, confused, stupid. And why are we constantly confused? Because we spend virtually all of our lives pointlessly wrapped up in our small self, under the spell of a rascal.

So even though we have an extremely fortunate life right now, we still go through a tremendous amount of suffering. It helps us to recognize this, not to make us feel sorry for ourselves, but to increase our motivation to be free. And though the suffering we experience every day is intense, we know too well that it could get much worse. Right now we are in a profoundly blessed situation, living in a place that isn't devastated by war, famine, lawlessness, or disease. There is no guarantee this will always be the case.

Even if we continue to have peaceful outer circumstances, we will still get old, get sick, and die. As we age, all our movements become more difficult. When you get old, as the great meditator Milarepa says, you start to walk like a child stalking a bird. You sit down like a heavy sack that has been cut from a rope and lands hard on the ground. You can't bend down and tie your shoes because your back hurts. It takes longer and longer to get out of bed because you're so stiff. Your digestive system gets weak, so much of the food you eat, instead of nourishing you, creates gas. You don't generate as much heat, so you feel cold even when wearing a lot of blankets. Socially you become more and more isolated. Diminished social contact dulls your mind. You start mumbling to yourself. You lose your memory, which you've always depended on to help you function in this world. You become more and more afraid about losing your abilities and independence. People start treating you like you're from another planet, as a being of another species who just resembles a human. You don't want to be a burden, but you need someone to rely on. But everyone is too busy. They all have their own lives to look after. They don't have time to visit you, and you can't go be with them because you don't fit into their world. And all of this you feel, right in your heart.

At some point you will become seriously ill. This could happen during old age or any time before. One day you go to the doctor for an exam. She has something to tell you. Immediately your heart starts to race. "Is it terminal?" The doctor isn't sure, but you will need more tests. Next thing you know, you're wearing hospital pajamas, surrounded by people wearing dresses and masks, carrying charts. They poke you with needles and take bottles and bottles of blood. They connect you to one machine after another. They won't let you eat. Before you know it, you're too weak to walk to the bathroom. Then they take you to the operation theater—machines and lights everywhere. They give you drugs to put you under. You have no choice. Slowly you fade away as you see knives and scissors, people with masks and gloves. While unconscious, you are taken apart and put back together. Your heart is replaced with an artificial pump. If you're lucky you may heal, but many dangers lie ahead. If the disease progresses, you will need more and more treatment. Things get more and more difficult. Soon you are on your deathbed, surrounded by loved ones. You look into their eyes. You can see that they know you're dying. But no one wants to talk about it. Everyone is clinging to hope. Finally it is time for you to die, to depart from this world alone, leaving behind all your loved ones and everything you worked so hard for. You don't want to let go, but there is no choice. You feel anxious and afraid. And if you've led a negative life, you feel terrified.

These contemplations may sound like exaggerations, but they only scratch the surface of our potential suffering. However intensely we reflect on the sufferings of samsara, we can't even come close to what beings actually go through. Imagine being an animal about to be slaughtered. You can't escape. You can't even speak. You have no control over what's happening to you. How would it feel to be a chicken about to have your head cut off, or a cow about to have your throat slit? How would it feel to be a crab in a tank at a restaurant, about to be boiled alive for someone's meal? You may think that these examples of other species don't apply to you. How could you ever end up in a pot of boiling water? But we have no idea what will happen to us after we die. We don't know what seeds we have planted and what will arise from them in future lives. This brings us to the fourth subject of contemplation: karma.

The Sanskrit word *karma* simply means "action." In a broader sense, the term is applied to the whole principle of cause and effect. In popular culture, karma is often thought to mean "fate" or "destiny," which are concepts that can make us feel helpless. On the contrary, understanding cause and effect empowers us to influence the course of our lives. In the short run, we can't always prevent the unfolding of results set in motion by many previous causes, but in the long run, if we plant favorable seeds, we will have increasingly favorable situations that will lead us all the way to enlightenment. When we know how to work with karma intentionally, as opposed to blindly allowing karma to carry us along, we can let go of our attachment to the present and our insecurity about the future.

But don't we already try to influence the future with our present actions? Don't we already look ahead, plan, and try to use our intelligence to make things turn out well? Yes, we do try and have always been trying. But it has never worked. This is where it's crucial to self-reflect with uncompromising honesty, not shying away because of embarrassment. We all want to be happy and free from suffering, but what we've done has almost always created the opposite results. There is no way around admitting this fact: we haven't mastered karma. This has nothing to do with being "bad," or being stained by original sin. If we feel guilty because our ignorance has led to bad things happening to us, then we're unlikely to self-reflect. We're more likely to conclude that "shit happens" for no reason. Temporarily this view may comfort us more than feeling responsible, but it will keep us stuck in helplessness. Unless we take the time to grapple with cause and effect and learn how to influence the future positively, we will always be victims.

So what should we do now that is different from everything we've tried in the past? The answer is simple. We step out of our small, singular self and embrace the limitless, universal self of all sentient beings. We generate bodhicitta and practice the exchange of self and other. In this life and in infinite past lives we've tried every conceivable method to achieve lasting happiness, but nothing has worked. Bodhicitta is the only thing we haven't tried, and bodhicitta happens to be the only method that does work.

But how do we know that bodhicitta is a positive cause leading to positive effects? What evidence is there that this is how karma operates? The Buddha gave us clear reasonings to determine whether an action is positive or negative, or in Buddhist terminology generates "merit" or "demerit." The first is that the result of positive actions, both long and short term, is happiness and freedom from suffering. Actions based on caring for the vast, universal self inevitably lead to joy; actions based on focusing on "me" perpetuate suffering.

The next reasoning is that actions focused on others and on ourselves, respectively, are *by their very nature* positive or negative, just as food by its very nature can be nourishing or toxic. At the moment you step out of the small self by applying the lojong teachings, at the moment you are engaged in positive thoughts and actions, your mind is in a state of peace and joy. Now sometimes we may think: "I try to do things for others, but it doesn't make me happy. Why?" This unhappiness doesn't come from doing things for others. That is a common misunderstanding. The suffering actually comes from our own self-centered attachment, based on not fully wanting to do what we're doing. If doing things for others caused suffering, then the bodhisattvas would be miserable. But their minds are full of peace because they are free from self-importance.

We may not like to think so much about others because we feel overwhelmed by their pain. We may think that developing compassion will make us suffer more. Turning our attention to what others are going through seems like self-inflicted—and probably pointless—torture. But we only fear this suffering because of our own self-cherishing. If we don't focus on and protect our small self, grossly exaggerating its significance, then there will be no one to get overwhelmed by the pain of others. If we truly embrace the universal self, we will have fearless and painless compassion, which will come with an immense wish and ability to benefit others. Understanding that caring for others is by its very nature peaceful and joyful helps us discern whether our true focus is on ourselves or on others. But if we find in this way that our focus is more on ourselves, we don't need to feel guilty or despondent (which in themselves are ways of clinging to the small self). Simply shift the focus by applying the lojong teachings, particularly the exchange of self and other, and you will find relief in your mind.

The Buddha's third reasoning is based on historical evidence. You can look at examples from the past and investigate whether self-importance has ever led to happiness or whether bodhicitta has ever led to suffering. The great sages have never found even one such counterexample. I don't think we will either. Sometimes people engaged in negativity, such as criminals who haven't been caught, seem to be doing well. But they are reaping their merit from the past, not benefiting from their present demerit. And even now, though it seems that fulfilling their greed has brought them satisfaction, are they really in a state of joy and peace? Would you say they are truly thriving?

Finally, practicing bodhicitta is clearly positive for social reasons. Our relationships with others improve and we become more in harmony with the world. Like flowers that naturally attract bees without any effort, bodhisattvas attract sentient beings whom they can care for and benefit. As a result, they are able to generate further and further merit and be of greater and greater benefit to the world. On the other hand, those who are driven mainly by self-interest find themselves more and more isolated, unable to reach others or to be reached.

When we practice mind training, we work with karma in the deepest way, accumulating merit and purifying our minds of what creates suffering. This all happens in our mental continuum: our present consciousness sows the seed and our future consciousness, whether in this life or the next, reaps the fruit. If we are careful to generate merit in this life, our mind will continue to enjoy peace and joy into our next life and we will create positive tendencies and circumstances that will lead us all the way to enlightenment.

Karma, the operation of cause and effect, is really the main theme of all the preliminary practices. When we contemplate precious human birth, impermanence, and suffering, it should be in the context of what we need to do to accumulate merit and purify our negativity. The four contemplations lay the groundwork for every other practice we do. They make all our spiritual efforts more precise and effective in transforming our lives.

Point Two

The Main Practice: Training in Bodhicitta

Absolute Bodhicitta

The practice of bodhicitta, the mind-set of awakening, includes two inseparable aspects: relative and absolute bodhicitta. Relative bodhicitta, which arises out of love and compassion, is the aspiration to attain enlightenment for the benefit of all sentient beings. Absolute bodhicitta is the direct insight into the empty nature of all phenomena. Though I have yet to come across a better term in English, the word *emptiness* has its drawbacks. It can frighten or disturb people and lead them to confuse Buddhism with nihilism. So it's important to state at the outset that emptiness doesn't refer to a void or a black hole. It is not the same as nonexistence. To say that a person or thing is "empty" simply means that it doesn't exist in the intrinsic way we think it does. When we say phenomena are empty, we mean that we can't grasp them or pin them down. It doesn't mean that they don't function or appear to our senses. I will go into more detail about this below.

Most teachings on bodhicitta begin with the relative aspect, since it is more accessible and easier to train in. In his *Seven Points,* however, Chekawa Yeshe Dorje begins with absolute bodhicitta. His reason is that if we can start off with some basic feel for emptiness, we can begin loosening our grasping to ourselves and phenomena as real. This will make our mind more agile and confident in applying the lojong practices that follow. For example, when practicing tonglen, knowing that suffering is ultimately illusory will give us the courage to take on the suffering of others. An introduction to emptiness will also increase our compassion for all the beings—the vast, vast majority of them—who don't even suspect that phenomena are not what they seem and therefore live a nightmarish existence. So even though we may not fully realize emptiness by studying these initial slogans, they help to set the tone for the entire path and to give us a sense of how deep our insights can go if we continue to practice.

Absolute Bodhicitta: In-Meditation

2. Consider all phenomena as a dream.

The absolute bodhicitta slogans give a step-by-step method for understanding emptiness at increasingly subtle levels. This slogan asks us to look into the characteristics of our dreams and see what they have in common with our waking experience. Dreams only occur under certain conditions. We can only experience a dream when we are asleep. This means that dreams aren't just "there" on their own. They only appear when a person is in a particular state of mind.

This is pretty obvious with dreams, but how does it relate to our waking experience? When we are asleep, our dreams affect us and convince us of their reality because we don't realize we're dreaming. Similarly, when we're awake, we are convinced that things are real because we don't realize we're misinterpreting what we perceive. Just as dreams are a function of our sleep, daytime phenomena are a function of our lack of understanding. During the day, we have various perceptions that we consider "reality." For example, we see a table. But our experience of the table is not based on seeing what's there. It's based on seeing what we *think* is there. We see the table as an unchanging object. Of course we're aware that at some point the table will get old or be destroyed, but for now we see today's table as the same as yesterday's and tomorrow's. But this is not true. In order for the table to gradually get old it must be changing every single instant. When we give this continuously changing phenomenon the name *table,* we are trying to pin down with language something that can't be pinned down. If a table never remains the same, even for an instant, it is always becoming a new object. When we utter the word *table,* the table that was there when we opened our mouth is different from the one that was there when we closed it. So which table does this word refer to? It's not that language is false or inherently problematic. Language is useful and necessary, but we need to recognize its limits. The conceptual mind can't fully describe or comprehend how things really are.

Another approach is to examine the subjective quality of our reality, whether we are asleep or awake. When we are asleep, our dream is *our* dream. It is never the dream of anyone else. We tend to think that our waking life is different, that we share a reality with others. True, there is some overlapping experience between beings with similar sense faculties and minds. But can we find one objective reality? Once I was sitting in a beautiful garden on a sunny day. Suddenly I noticed a bit of cat poop right in front of me. I felt disgusted, especially when I realized that it was partially squashed and that I might have stepped on it. I was thinking about getting rid of it, but I also didn't want to touch it. So I was at a loss. Then I noticed that a fly was enjoying the poop tremendously. It was shocking to see how the whole problem—the dirtiness, the offensive smell—was all in my mind, all a projection. The fly was a great teacher for me. It reminded me how everything is like this; all experience is nothing other than our mind's subjective experience. For you and me, a glass of water is something to drink. For a fish, it could be a home. Even two people looking at the "same" object see different things, depending on their eyesight, or what characteristics they tend to notice, or where they are standing. In themselves things have no intrinsic nature.

In dreams none of the phenomena that appear to us have any substance. But this is also true for waking life. Look at something as unmistakably solid as a brick wall. A brick wall is made of individual bricks. We can keep breaking these pieces down until they become as fine as dust. If we continue to analyze, we will see that each dust particle is made up of atoms. Each atom consists of a nucleus of protons and neutrons orbited by electrons. Relative to the space taken up by the atom, the nucleus is extremely tiny. Since the electrons are far away from the nucleus, most of the atom's volume is completely empty. Then, if the nucleus itself is taken apart, we will find even more space within. If we take the analysis to its ultimate conclusion, we will find smaller and smaller particles surrounded by space, and eventually nothing but space. The brick wall that stands vividly before our eyes is made entirely of space.

At first, this type of contemplation may not have a lot of practical impact on our everyday life. After all, even if we "know" a brick wall is made of space, we can't walk through it. Our habit of seeing objects as solid is too tenacious to change after a few contemplations. This analysis, however, can be practical immediately if we apply it to our own minds, especially to the five main painful emotions that bewilder, torment, and overwhelm us throughout our lives. The five poisons—attachment, aggression, jealousy, arrogance, and stupidity—have so much power over us that it's hard to believe they are mere illusions. But if they truly exist, where are they?

Let's go back to the cat poop. When I first smelled it, the emotion of aggression arose in my mind. Though it was a relatively mild form of aggression, there is no question that I wanted that poop out of my happy garden scene. But can I locate that aggression? Does it exist inherently within the cat poop? If it did, then the fly would also experience aggression. Does the aggression dwell somewhere between the poop and my nose? That doesn't make sense, for how can aggression just be hanging out somewhere in space? Maybe the aggression exists in the place where I become aware of the smell, perhaps where my nose connects to my brain and my consciousness. But that also can't be, because my nose is always connected to my brain, but I don't always have an aggression toward a smell. Is there anywhere else the aggression could exist? Where could that be?

After searching high and low, we find that an aggression toward a bad smell is nothing but an illusion produced by certain conditions coming together. It's like a rainbow that appears when all the right factors (sun, rain, the perspective of the viewer) come together. But a rainbow, just like an object in a dream, and just like a disturbing emotion, doesn't exist in any solid way, or in any particular place. It is just a passing effect. With this kind of exploration, we can discover that everything that comes up in our mind, everything that bothers us or makes us anxious, has no substance whatsoever. None of our thoughts and emotions have any essence. When we see them for what they are, mere dreamlike appearances, they lose their power to disturb us and to cause us to act in ways that perpetuate our suffering. By training ourselves to see these phenomena as dreams, we can stop being intimidated by our own mind.

3. Examine the nature of unborn awareness.

Once we have applied the above analysis and tasted the illusory nature of phenomena, we look at our mind itself. Is our mind also illusory? Or is there something there, something real?

To investigate, we should simply turn our attention inward and look at this mind. See whether it has any form, shape, color, anything we can pinpoint. Is there anything we can put a finger on and say "This is my mind" or "This is my awareness"? Does our mind have a place of origin? Does it have a location? When each mental experience ends, does it go to any particular place? We can look and look, but we will never find affirmative answers to any of these questions. If we keep searching, eventually we'll be convinced. Then we will see for ourselves what the great meditators have discovered: "Not finding is finding." Why can't we find any of these characteristics to our mind? Because our mind is like space. Space is primordial; there was never a time before space came into being. Therefore we say that space is "unborn." In the same way, our mind, our awareness, is primordial. Because we can never find our awareness, we can't say there was ever a time when our awareness didn't exist and was then born. This is the meaning of "unborn awareness."

4. The antidote in itself is liberated.

When we gain this basic understanding that mind is unborn, that it has no characteristics, that it is "empty," an interesting thing often happens. Because we have discovered something important, remarkable, and in line with the most profound Buddhist teachings, we want to hold on to this realization. We know that our mind and all phenomena are illusory, and we want to maintain that knowledge. Seeing, for example, that all our painful emotions are unreal is the most powerful antidote to suffering. So having this incentive, we tend to cling to our view of emptiness in subtle ways. When we have a glimpse of emptiness, we try to hold on to it and make that experience continue. We may even try to create some kind of emptiness in our mind. Of course it is not actual emptiness, but our idea of emptiness.

At that point, we need to take a step back and look at this clinging to our idea of emptiness. What is that experience? Is there anything we can really find or pinpoint? We can also look at the mind that experiences or clings to emptiness. Does that experiencer or clinger have any shape or color, any characteristics whatsoever? No matter how hard you look, you won't be able to find any kind of reality to this grasping mind.

5. Rest in the nature of the alaya.

Through this investigation, our *idea* of emptiness will eventually fade away and we'll be left simply with our unborn wakeful state of mind, free from all of our usual grasping to concepts. It is a state of mind that there's no language for, since language is based on concepts. In this state, our mind is free from all pinpointing and clinging to reality. Since our mind grasps at nothing, any thoughts that arise are instantly self-liberated. They simply melt into space. This space, which is not a void but is pervaded by enlightened awareness, is called the *alaya*.

The word *alaya* has different definitions based on context. It often refers to an underlying dullness in our mind that is the source of all our deluded experience. In this slogan, however, alaya refers to the enlightened nature that all beings with a mind possess. The bodhisattva's ultimate aim is to realize this state of alaya and to bring all other beings to that same realization.

Absolute Bodhicitta: Post-Meditation
6. In post-meditation, be a child of illusion.

Outside of our formal meditation practice, when we are engaged with the world and all our activities, we should reflect on the four slogans above and connect to absolute bodhicitta. For short moments, here and there, we can try to see the world without concepts, the way a small child does. We can pretend we're having a lucid dream or that the world is like a movie that appears on the screen and then disappears. The speed of modern life can enhance this practice. Everything happens so fast our senses can't register it all. We can't really notice and capture what's happening before our eyes. If our mind is awake rather than tuned out, we can use this vivid experience of transience to reduce our attachment and aggression in relation to phenomena.

Being a child of illusion doesn't impede our ability to function in the world. We will still know when we have to eat and when we have to go to the bathroom. We won't just check out, removing ourselves to our own private world. The great sages who have realized this view are able to function much more effectively than we can, bringing immense benefit to other beings. But they do so without having any sense that their activities are real.

Relative Bodhicitta

By studying and contemplating the slogans on absolute bodhicitta, we may gain an inkling of emptiness and our enlightened nature. This may give us a sense of what kind of freedom we will achieve in our minds if we follow this path. It will also give us a sense of the freedom that all other sentient beings have as their potential and birthright. But Lama Serlingpa, Atisha's most revered teacher, warns us about prematurely overemphasizing the absolute. He says that focusing too much on emptiness at first can make it hard to give birth to a genuine wish to attain enlightenment for the benefit of all beings. As it says in one of the sutras, "The lotus does not grow out of dry land; only from wet, muddy land, can the lotus bloom." We can't immediately transcend our suffering by connecting to and staying in our absolute nature. Only by getting to know how we cherish and protect our small self can we gradually step out of that narrow view and embrace the universal self. Then, as Jamgon Kongtrul says, "With the development of relative bodhicitta, absolute bodhicitta is naturally realized."

Relative Bodhicitta: In-Meditation

7. Practice giving and taking alternately.
Mount both upon the breath.

Of all the practices for stepping out of the small self, none is more profound or effective than the exchange of self and other. As Shantideva says in *The Way of the Bodhisattva*, "Unless you don't want to attain enlightenment, you must practice tonglen." He goes on to say that it will even be hard to find peace in our conventional lives without the exchange of self and other. Therefore, tonglen—whether in the specific form of using breath as a medium, or in the various other ways of exchanging self and other—is the heart of lojong, and the heart of the *Seven Points*. In fact, Jamgon Kongtrul goes so far as to say that "other approaches to mind training are mere elaborations" of the exchange of self and other.

But before embarking on the practice of exchange, it's important to put it into context and be clear *why* we're doing such a thing. It may seem unnatural or even unhealthy to lessen our self-cherishing and transfer that cherishing to others. If we force ourselves to do it without understanding how it works and why it makes sense, we may only increase the disturbance in our mind. As we have seen, self-importance is the root of all our troubles in life, from our moment-to-moment anxieties and insecurities, to all the external circumstances that disturb our minds. When we train in the preliminaries, we begin to connect the dots between self-importance and negative karma. This gives us incentive to do something about the rascal in our heart.

To counteract the rascal, we arouse bodhicitta, the wish to attain enlightenment for the sake of all beings. Then we progressively practice in three stages. First, we contemplate the equality of ourselves and others. This enables us to practice tonglen, the exchange of self and other. Finally, we train ourselves to care for others more than ourselves. This three-part process has tremendous wisdom and power to transform our minds. Once we have learned this wisdom, we execute it precisely in our body, speech, and mind.

THE EQUALITY OF SELF AND OTHER

I have already brought up this theme in the introduction. Now let's look at it in more depth. Go to a quiet place and settle your mind. Then look within and tune in to your wish for your own happiness. Try to look at your mind objectively, without judgment. You will find that your desire for happiness is with you every second of every day. You are always longing for happiness, deeply and intensely. And you are always trying to *do* something, either externally or within your own thought process, to bring about this happiness, in big or small ways. You may go through times when you are hard on yourself, when you think you don't like yourself. You may even be full of self-loathing. But even in those times, don't assume you're not concerned with your own happiness. You still want to drink something if you're thirsty, or get warm if you're cold, or go to sleep if you're tired. The desire for happiness, and whatever you think brings about happiness, never leaves you.

All the while that you are seeking happiness, you are simultaneously trying to get away from any form of suffering. You do not want any physical, emotional, or mental suffering to come near you. When faced with even the smallest suffering, such as a tiny insect bite, you try to avoid it. You also try your best to escape anything that might eventually lead to suffering. Of course, we all cause ourselves suffering all the time, but that is not because we accept pain. We find pain and suffering to be totally unacceptable. But we don't connect the dots and see how the very actions designed to lead to our happiness in fact bring about the opposite effect. Look into your own experience and see whether this is true.

Now think about the experience of other sentient beings. Is there a single one of them who is different? Is any being, at this moment, not concerned with his, her, or its happiness and freedom from suffering? You can't literally get inside the mind of another being, but you can still examine these questions and see what makes sense to you. Watch an ant moving toward sugar or away from fire. Isn't that an indication of these desires? In Tibetan, we say that all beings with a mind are *drowa semchen,* which means "moving beings." Where are we moving? We are all moving, unceasingly, toward what we think will bring us happiness, and away from what we think will make us suffer. No matter how different we look or act, no matter how intelligent or stupid we are, all of us are moving beings. This impulse to move is the very core of our being. Everything else about us, every other characteristic we consider part of this "self," is temporary, brought about by impermanent and unpredictable causes and conditions. Therefore, in our very essence, we are all identical. This is worth thinking about for a long time, until it becomes completely clear in our minds. When we vividly and unmistakably see our equality with others, the rest of the bodhicitta practices become much more natural and straightforward.

Contemplating our essential equality with all other beings helps us develop a bond with them in our minds. Usually we are intensely concerned with our own desires and those of our loved ones. But beyond that small population, there are infinite sentient beings outside the circle of our care. What determines who is inside or outside this circle? Nothing but self-importance. You may love your children deeply. You may be willing to sacrifice all your personal happiness for them. But is that love completely selfless? No, because its basis is *you*. If your love were free of self-importance, then it wouldn't matter if these children were yours or not. All that would matter would be your understanding that these are sentient beings who want to be happy and free from suffering just as much as you do.

Right now this way of thinking may seem remote and idealistic, but that is only because it's not our mind's habit. Seeing that ourselves and all other beings are identical at our core helps break down the habitual division between self and other. The very terms *self* and *other* start to become less solid. If another being is, in essence, exactly like me, how is that being really "other"? If my child and a child in a foreign country are, at their innermost level, the same, why should there be a difference in my care for them? The dividing line between self and other is simply based on habits we've established. Before we were conceived, we were a disembodied consciousness looking for a home. Inside our future mother was an egg; inside our future father were some sperm. When one of the sperm entered our mother and fertilized the egg, our consciousness discovered its home. That moment was the beginning of our present life's habit to regard a chunk of matter and its associated consciousness as "me." Though the matter has changed dramatically (we don't bear the faintest resemblance to a fertilized egg), and though our consciousness is never the same for an instant, the habit of clinging to this vague sense of self persists.

But because the mind is infinitely malleable, even the strongest habits can be changed. The habit of self-importance is no exception. The classic Tibetan example involves a deal with a horse. When someone wants to sell a horse, the well-being of that horse is solely his concern. If the horse suddenly develops colic before the deal is made, the seller will have all the worry over whether it will survive. But as soon as the horse is sold, anything that happens to it becomes the new owner's problem. This shows how quickly one's mind and reactions can change once there's a shift in responsibility or a transfer of money. Changing what we cling to as a self, however, doesn't come about through an economic transaction. It happens through mind training.

If we start to think of all other beings as "ours," simply because we see that they are essentially just like ourselves and our loved ones in their longing for happiness and freedom from suffering, then we will naturally grow to feel concern and responsibility for each and every one. A story from the Buddha's childhood illustrates this beautifully. Once the Buddha's jealous cousin Devadatta shot down a swan with an arrow. He went to retrieve the wounded bird, only to find that she had fallen into the Buddha's lap. Devadatta approached the Buddha and asked him to surrender the swan, saying she was his. According to the conventional view, this was true. But the Buddha refused to give him the swan, saying that for many lifetimes he had trained his mind to regard all beings as *his,* though in a different way. They were his not to own, but to protect. It was for that reason that the swan had landed in the Buddha's lap. The Buddha and his cousin each presented their case before the royal ministers and the Buddha's father, King Suddhodana. In the end they concluded that the Buddha's claim had more weight. The Buddha cared for the swan until her wound had healed and she could fly away.

Like the Buddha, we're all capable of spreading our love infinitely, simply by using our own familiar concern for ourselves as a reference point. Now you may think, "There's only one of me, there are only a few of my loved ones, but the number of living beings is countless. It's unrealistic to spread my love that far. It's even beyond my capacity to imagine." It is true that the number of beings is countless. But we can still develop the habit of seeing them as all part of a universal self. We already have a similar habit of clinging to an innumerable and extremely varied collection as a self. Our arms, legs, heart, lungs, eyes, teeth, hair, bones, muscles, nerves, blood, cells, thoughts, emotions, personality, character, intelligence, and so on: we see all of these parts as "me." Everyone does this, without a problem. Even though that fertilized egg started out so basic and grew more and more complicated as our body developed, we've had no problem expanding our concern to keep up with this multitude of new and changing parts. We love this collection that we call "me" as a whole. This is natural, not logically impossible. In the same manner, we can train our mind to love all beings as a whole, collectively.

You may then say it's not practical to love an infinite number of sentient beings. Look at what is involved with loving just one infant! But love can't always be tied to immediate action. This practice we are talking about is for developing your heart. To put love into action requires having the right circumstances. Right now you may be in a situation to only benefit your children, or your parents, or your pet. The conditions that bring about the right circumstances are mostly beyond your control. By the same token, though you feel concern for your body as a whole, you may not see any opportunity (or reason) to do something for any one small part. But if your gall bladder malfunctions and it's possible for you to cure the problem, then you will do all you can to help that organ, even if that particular body part had never before come into your mind. Similarly, if you have developed a love for all beings in your heart, when the right situations do come about, you will respond actively and skillfully to help individuals. The more you deepen your *zhen che dzin,* your altruistic concern for others, the greater and wider practical benefit you will bring to them.

By contemplating the equality of our self and others, we can gradually expand the circle of our care until our wish for all others' happiness is as great as our wish for our own. This may seem like a remote aspiration, but if we don't stretch our wings, we won't know how big they are. A young king is limited in his power. If there is an earthquake in his country, he can go to the site of the destruction and show his concern. He can't immediately rebuild all the houses, but he does whatever he can, to the extent of his current ability. This is the mark of a good young king. He is concerned about his country, he does what he can, and he works to develop his ability to benefit others. In the same way, we can think of ourselves, whatever age we are, as young bodhisattvas who have been assigned to lead countless sentient beings—ultimately all sentient beings—to liberation from samsara. Because of our habit of clinging to a small self, our ability and vision are limited. But if we make it a priority to reduce our self-importance and focus more on the happiness of others, we are off to a good start. From there, our bodhicitta will expand naturally and inevitably.

TONGLEN: THE EXCHANGE OF SELF AND OTHER

Seeing the equality of self and other paves the way for the main practice of tonglen. Once we begin to see that self and other are essentially no different, making the exchange doesn't seem so unnatural or difficult. Tonglen is divided into four types of exchange: (1) exchange of affection for intolerance; (2) exchange of position; (3) exchange of happiness for suffering; and (4) exchange of merit for demerit.

Exchange of Affection for Intolerance—The first kind of tonglen is the most important because it is the ground for the other three. If we can't make this kind of basic exchange, then the rest of the practices will be as painful as undergoing dental surgery without an anesthetic. In this exchange, we give to others the strong affection we usually reserve for ourselves and our close ones. Instead of focusing our care on ourselves, we focus it on others. Instead of thinking and feeling, "I am so dear to myself," we think and feel, "All other beings are so dear to me." We give them every bit of cherishing we normally lavish on ourselves. It is natural now to have some hesitations. You may think to yourself, "Others do indeed want happiness and freedom from suffering as much as I do. That makes sense. Others are indeed dear to me. I have no problem feeling affection for them. But what about me? Shouldn't I reserve some affection for me?"

At this point it is important to clarify who it is that is giving away the affection. We are not trying to punish ourselves with this practice. Tonglen isn't a form of martyrdom. When I practice tonglen, I do not think, "May Dzigar Kongtrul fall into the depths of misery because he is such a horrible, unworthy person." That is not the purpose at all. Then who is it that we are stripping of affection so that it can be given to all other sentient beings? That one is none other than our tendency to cling to a small self—our self-importance. You *should* have affection for yourself as an embodiment of bodhicitta, the wish to attain enlightenment for the benefit of all beings. You should care for the person who sees that self and other are equal, for the person who is essentially inseparable from all sentient beings. But is there any reason to keep coddling the spoiled-rotten rascal who has caused all your suffering in samsara? Is there any reason to keep nourishing your archenemy, self-importance?

This is the true meaning of taking away our affection for ourselves and giving it to others. If you ever find yourself using tonglen as a way to beat yourself up, please pause and remind yourself that that is not the aim. Guilt and self-aggression are actually forms of self-importance in disguise. Instead of letting go of the small self, you make a huge deal about it. Guilt arises from a powerful and disturbing feeling that you *should* be a better person. You want to be "good" all the time, but it's impossible because being that good takes a lot of mind training, a lot of self-reflection and working with your habitual tendencies. Either you don't know how to do this work, you don't want to do this work, or you feel that it's beyond you. So instead you focus on how bad you are, how intrinsically bad. But as we have seen, the core of every sentient being's mind is the wish to be happy and free from suffering. This core is completely innocent. All the harmful thoughts and emotions that often dominate our minds are the product of causes and conditions that we have little or no control over. In this way, there is no such thing as being intrinsically "good" or "bad." The much more meaningful distinction is between "confused" and "clear."

Being clear on these points is also crucial for performing the other half of this first type of exchange. As the word implies, *tonglen* involves giving something to others and taking something on to oneself. In this case, when we give others our affection, what are we taking on?

Toward those who are outside our circle of affection, °we tend to feel indifference or aversion. We have varying degrees of intolerance, from gross to subtle, toward those we regard as "other." But since we have contemplated the fact that others are essentially no different from ourselves, such intolerance makes no sense. Instead of directing it outward, we can make better use of our intolerance by taking it on ourselves, which again means directing it toward our self-importance. This attachment to a small self, the cause of all suffering, is the only worthy recipient of our intolerance. But again we must make sure that this intolerance comes from critical intelligence, not from emotional reactivity or guilt.

Exchange of Position—Once we have established this basis of being able to exchange affection for intolerance, we can practice the next three types of tonglen. The next method, the exchange of position, is a specific antidote to three of our most disturbing emotions: arrogance, competitiveness, and jealousy. This ingenious practice, which comes from the Meditation chapter in Shantideva's *Way of the Bodhisattva*, uses the emotions themselves as an antidote to self-importance.

In each variation, put yourself in the shoes of someone looking at yourself. In my case, I would imagine myself looking at "Dzigar Kong-trul," who is now an outsider. Identify with the other person and all of his or her emotions. Drop your allegiance to your habitual self (Kong-trul) and see him as a problem in your life.

The first step is to imagine that you are in an inferior position and are thus prone to jealousy. Vent your emotions to the superior person who thinks he is better than you: "You (Kongtrul) have it all, while I have nothing. You are so privileged, while I am destitute. You are praised and admired; I am ignored and left alone. I feel so angry and jealous because of what you have and I don't. If you cared for me, if you were generous with me, then I could respect you. I might even be happy for you. But you don't care for me or try to help me in any way. All you do is look down on me, with all your arrogance. So why should

I have any good feelings toward you? Why should I be happy about what you have?" Seeing yourself from the jealous person's point of view is an effective antidote to arrogance. Instead of feeling smugly superior to the other person, you will grow to understand the suffering of others and develop compassion and tolerance.

Next put yourself in the position of a more equal rival looking at yourself (Kongtrul): "I'm going to compete with you, and, what's more, I'm going to win. I don't intend to win just once, I mean to win every time, and deprive you of any possibility of winning. I will hide your good qualities from the world and do everything in my power to prevent people from recognizing them. But all my good qualities, I'll proclaim to the world and I'll feast upon the recognition I deserve. Your faults I will publicize, but my faults I will bury so that nobody even catches a glimpse of them." Bringing out the ugliness of rivalry in such an explicit way undermines our small-minded tendency to be competitive. Seeing it in such a harsh light can provoke us to lean toward the opposite behavior. Since we have some experience with the first type of tonglen, the exchange of affection, we can now behave more in a way that benefits others while shrinking our self-importance. Instead of proclaiming our own good qualities and publicizing the faults of others, we can proclaim the good qualities of others and make known (at least to ourselves) all the faults of our own grasping to the small self.

Then put yourself in the position of someone who is superior to you and feels arrogant about that. "You (Kongtrul) are so pathetic, thinking you can compete with me, when I have all these good qualities and you have none. It makes me laugh that you could even dare to think you're my equal! I'm rich, beautiful, intelligent, talented. Everyone knows how great I am. What do you have going for you? Nothing. So on what basis are you comparing yourself with me? If you behave yourself and do what I want you to do, then maybe I'll show you a little respect. But be careful because I can take away that respect whenever I like."

When you do this practice, you will wonder what the point is of comparing yourself with others when it leads to this kind of dynamic. This other person does indeed have good qualities, but how can they enjoy them when they're so immersed in arrogance? Why be jealous, when the person on the other side is suffering so much from their own self-importance? Furthermore, why should you resent the superior person's low opinion of you? What is the actual object of their contempt? It isn't your innate wish to be happy and free from suffering. Both of you have that wish as your core. It isn't your bodhicitta, which is in the process of waking up to its full potential for the benefit of all sentient beings. If someone has a low opinion of you, that low opinion is only based on your self-importance, the source of every sentient being's faults. So why feel bad about yourself? Why let yourself be consumed with jealousy? Why not take this opportunity of being "inferior" to expose and wear away your attachment to the small self? You can also recognize that the other's arrogance is a natural complement to your jealousy. Sensing your jealousy gives others an unpleasant feeling, which provokes their behavior and leads to both of you suffering.

Exchange of Happiness for Suffering—Now we come to the practice sequence most commonly associated with the word *tonglen*. There are many versions of this practice, but all of them involve imagining one or more beings who are suffering, and performing an exchange based on one's breath. As we breathe in, we imagine ourselves taking on their suffering. Breathing out, we imagine ourselves giving them our happiness.

Go to a quiet place and sit up straight, in a position where you feel calm and comfortable. Start by visualizing your mother in front of you, clearly and vividly, just as she is or was, just as you know her. Think to yourself, "I am going to meditate on love and compassion with my mother as the object." Think like this:

My mother has given me this precious human birth, and thanks to her gift, I have come in contact with the noble dharma. I have been able to start on the path of enlightenment; from this point on, I will be on a path of increasing bliss and happiness. This is all due to her. She has provided me with this immense benefit. Even when I was inside her body, she nurtured and cared for me. After I was born, until I was on my own, she cared for me in so many different ways, bringing me all the benefits anyone could think of. It is likely that this mother has been with me not just in this lifetime, but in many past lifetimes, throughout my beginningless existence in samsara. Her affectionate, kind eyes have always looked warmly upon me. She holds me constantly in her heart with affection and kindness. She is always worried about me. She has protected me from countless dangers and threats. Any benefit that I enjoy in the world is due to her. I am so grateful for what she has done for me, who she is to me, and what she means to me.

Reflect deeply in this way, recalling the various acts of kindness that your mother has done for you until tears fall from your eyes, until your whole body tingles, until your consciousness is transformed. Then, think:

This mother of mine who has been so immensely kind and compassionate, who has benefitted me so much, is now wandering in samsara. She will wander indefinitely. And she is wandering because of me. In caring for, worrying about, thinking about her child, her heart is completely occupied. She endures so much suffering and pain from this. How sad! How sad that she will continue to wander in samsara! I will generate heartfelt sympathy and compassion toward her. I will earnestly wish for her to be free from suffering and free from samsara.

Guide your thoughts and emotions in this manner again and again until your heart melts into compassion, until an abundance of deep appreciation and a feeling of deep closeness arises in your heart. Then continue by thinking to yourself:

Now I must do something significant to repay her kindness. I must do for her what she has done for me: protect her from all threats and fears, and all the suffering that she may endure. I must bring her the benefits of goodness, of all that is worthy.

Think about what will harm her more than any other harm. This is the suffering of samsara: birth, old age, sickness, and death—with all their attendant hopes, disappointments, rejections, anxieties, and fears. And where do these come from? The five poisons of attachment, aggression, jealousy, arrogance, and stupidity, which in turn come from the source of all suffering: self-importance. So say to yourself:

I will take upon myself all these sensations of my mother's suffering, both physical and emotional, as well as their causes. I will take on all the habitual tendencies, all the gross and subtle levels of her insecurity and fear. I will remove them as if they were her clothes, and I will wear them myself. I will completely relieve her burden and take it instead as my own. I will take it right into my heart.

Think also:

I will protect her. I will deliver to her all the pleasures, joy, and happiness in the world. I will give my own cherished body to her in service. I will give all my possessions, all that I hold as belonging to me, including all my virtuous acts. Without any stinginess, without any conditions, I will offer it all to her. Emulating Shantideva's prayer in The Way of the Bodhisattva, *I will aspire to become a wish-fulfilling jewel for the benefit of others. I will imagine all that she needs and diligently offer it to her—service, belongings, wealth, virtue—like a wish-fulfilling jewel. I will bring about all the circumstances for her to realize the truth. I will provide her with food and clothes, teacher and teachings, so she can set out on the path of truth. Then through the accumulation of her own merit, may she attain enlightenment.*

While generating abundant love and compassion toward your own mother, use your breath to give and take alternately. As your mind softens, do this practice more and more from the depth of your heart. In this way, for the sake of your own mother—for her happiness and protection—you should feel that you actually give up all your attachment to the small self. If you found her in the flames of hell, you could, without any hesitation, jump into the fire to bring her out. When such strength and courage are engendered in your heart, you will know you have done the practice well.

That is the first part of the formal practice of tonglen. The second part is to think of all sentient beings as your mothers, and generate love and compassion in a similar way:

From beginningless time, I have taken birth after birth and been cared for by infinite mothers. Every sentient being has at one time or another been my mother. Therefore, I must commit myself to dedicating my life to all my mother sentient beings. I commit myself to giving away all my attachments, and to surrendering them to all my kind mothers. I will give away all my possessions, all that belongs to me, and all my virtuous acts. Infinite numbers of sentient beings exist throughout limitless space, and I alone will bring them all to the point of liberation. I've made this commitment and will bear it on my shoulders. I will do this immediately and deliberately, with great care.

This is the way you should do the tonglen practice for all mother sentient beings: taking on all their suffering, and giving all that you can—all that you have—transforming yourself into a wish-fulfilling jewel for the benefit of beings. When you give away all that belongs to you—your body, possessions, and merit—visualize everyone enjoying it equally. No one will lack anything. Give completely, from the depth of your heart, without any stinginess or conditions, totally letting it go. Ask beings to take whatever they want from you, thinking, "Please use all this to enjoy yourself. Make whatever use of it you like." Consider yourself a wish-fulfilling jewel, a medicinal tree that can heal all the desires and needs of beings. Anything that you have, that you're attached to, that you hold tightly—give it all away without hesitation, from the depth of your detachment. Recite these words:

My body, my possessions, my belongings, my virtue and merit, all in abundance, I give away to my mother sentient beings: as their food to eat, as their drink to drink, as belongings for those who have nothing, as a resting place for those who have nowhere to rest. In samsara and nirvana, whatever happiness and causes of happiness are found, may I alone serve to bring them to all mother sentient beings. May I alone take upon myself all the suffering and pain of the world and samsara. May I alone be the patron assisting all mother sentient beings to find the path of dharma and its fruition. May all that they need come from me alone.

Recite this again and again. Then consider this:

All the buddhas of the past, present, and future have in their hearts nothing but the wish to serve beings. The priority in every bodhisattva's heart is to serve beings. How wonderful and joyous it is to have this opportunity right now. How wonderful it is to be able to do this, just as I am.

All my companions on the path—whatever obscurations and hindrances remain for them, may I be able to take them upon myself. May they thus become free of all hindrances and obscurations, accumulate merit immediately, and attain enlightenment.

In this way, you give and take, mounting these actions on your breath. As you breathe in, you can imagine that the suffering of others comes as darkness that dissolves into your heart. As you breathe out, imagine your happiness in the form of light rays radiating from your nostrils and being absorbed by every sentient being. Using the breath and the visualization helps keep the mind focused and prevents it from drifting into irrelevant or destructive thoughts.

In his commentary, Jamgon Kongtrul emphasizes feeling joy while doing this practice. Joy is the key to tonglen. It has to be the motivating factor in both giving and taking. When you do something for a loved one, even if it brings you some pain or hardship, your joy generally overrides that hardship. So when you practice tonglen and imagine taking on another's suffering, really try to feel the great joy that would come from that person's relief. If a mother could take on her child's fever and remove all feelings of sickness from her child, imagine the great joy she would feel. Similarly, when you give away your happiness, feel the vicarious joy in another's receiving it. Think about how happy a mother is when her child gains any sort of happiness, and enjoy that feeling of satisfaction.

Practicing with joy is a much more effective approach than being confused and doubtful, wondering whether we are just playing a foolish game. If we just go through the motions, thinking that this practice won't really benefit ourselves or others, then it won't penetrate our self-importance. It won't reverse our habit of cherishing and protecting the small self, which is the cause of all our suffering. Instead of having this impoverished attitude to our practice, we should reflect on how magnificent and skillful tonglen is. This is the most sacred practice of all the buddhas and bodhisattvas, and somehow we have found ourselves with the great fortune to have it in our lives.

Tonglen is an outrageous idea. When we're in pain, our natural reaction is to free ourselves from suffering, not take on more. It almost seems masochistic. Sometimes people fear this practice of exchange because they think that mentally taking on the sufferings of others will make bad things happen to them: "Will mentally taking on someone's disease make me get sick?" This is not something we need to fear. The cause of all our pain in life is negative karma from the past. Negative karma is the direct result of our acting on behalf of a small self at the expense of others. Another being's suffering can't literally be transferred into ourselves when there is no karmic basis for that to happen. From time to time, when the conditions are right, a bodhisattva who has completely stepped out of the small self can literally take on another's suffering. But we are not yet at that level. When we take on others' suffering, we don't literally get stricken with their pain. We don't have to be dramatic, reducing this practice to emotionalism.

Because of its altruistic motivation, tonglen only sows the seeds for positive results to arise in the future. And in the present, it brings about our well-being by purifying the seeds of our suffering and shortening its duration. By mentally adding to the suffering we're already experiencing, we loosen our grasping to the small self, thereby reducing our self-importance. Through the power and blessing of compassion and bodhicitta, tonglen actually results in our being relieved from suffering. We may still have our habitual patterns, but their power is lessened by the radical change in how we relate, psychologically and emotionally, to our pain.

Since working conceptually with each of our mental activities is an endless process, we must get to the root of the problem. If we remedy the root cause of our suffering, we simultaneously remedy whatever arises from that root. Of all the practices available to us, this exchange of happiness for suffering is the one that most effectively and precisely penetrates to the root. If we put it into practice, we will benefit immensely.

Exchange of Merit for Demerit—In this last form of exchange, we mentally give others all the merit from our past positive deeds, and we take on all the demerit from others' negativity. Merit is the karmic result from actions based on others' welfare. From this perspective, it is the source of all the goodness in our lives. For this reason, we can easily cling to our merit, thinking of it as our most valuable "possession." But the irony is that such an attitude only increases our self-importance and therefore brings us demerit. So the practice here is to mentally give all our positive karma to others. We try to give it away freely and joyfully, with great satisfaction. And at the same time, we take others' wrongdoings, disturbing emotions, ignorance, and obscurations upon ourselves, feeling happy to provide such relief. As with the other types of exchange, this counterintuitive practice goes against the conventional idea about what is in our best interest. But when we reverse our habitual self-clinging, we actually increase our merit by giving it away, while protecting ourselves from negativity by taking it on!

We can expand our offering infinitely, by adding all the merit accumulated by the buddhas and bodhisattvas of the past, present, and future. Since they have dedicated all their merit for the benefit of others, we can feel free to offer it on their behalf. It's as if they've given us power of attorney to access their immense bank account and use it for whatever altruistic purpose we desire. Since this merit is so vast, we can imagine that, as soon as it reaches our mother sentient beings, they instantly accomplish the entire path and become completely enlightened. As a result samsara is emptied forever. Believing that our practice of exchange is actually contributing to such an outcome fills us with great joy.

CARING FOR OTHERS MORE THAN OURSELVES

After contemplating the equality of self and other and practicing tonglen comes the third stage in this sequence of mind training. When we practice and familiarize ourselves with equality and exchange, we already have one foot in the door of caring for others more than ourselves. For as we make progress along the bodhisattva's path, we start to discover that there is not really anything to accomplish for ourselves. Our whole endeavor in life is to benefit others.

The most highly evolved bodhisattvas no longer have any fear or concern for themselves. They are not even concerned about giving up their lives. The Buddha, in a previous life, is said to have given his own flesh and bone to a starving tiger so that she would have sustenance to feed her cubs. We are not at that stage yet, but we can admire and applaud such stories of courage and aspire to give birth to the freedom, strength, and fearlessness that arise from bodhicitta. We can aspire to serve sentient beings without the slightest fear, attachment, or regret. And we can develop our minds to value others' liberation from suffering more than our own.

Reaching this level of selflessness is not as farfetched as it sounds. For countless eons in samsara, we have already endured suffering after suffering, usually without any great motivation, much less the supreme motivation of bodhicitta. As Nagarjuna says, if we collected all the limbs we have ever lost, they would make a pile bigger than the highest mountain. If we gathered all the tears we've shed, they would make a body of water greater than all the world's oceans. Think of all the soldiers who give their lives for their country. Think of what a farmer goes through in one year. Think of the effort it takes to go through decades of education to become a doctor or lawyer. Then think of how much benefit these exertions and sacrifices have had, especially in the long run. If we had put this kind of effort into an activity with great vision, into training our minds and progressing on the bodhisattva's path, we would be far along by now. The idea of caring for other beings—all other beings—more than ourselves would seem a lot more familiar and natural. Having the freedom to give others anything we own, without the least hesitation, would seem like the greatest bliss.

For beginner bodhisattvas like ourselves, giving away our body parts is expressly prohibited by the Buddhist teachings. Even smaller acts of self-sacrifice, if they are beyond our current level, are not necessarily the best way to go. For example, say you and your two children have hiked to the top of a mountain. All three of you are hungry. You look in your backpack and only find one apple. If you're motivated by altruism, you will cut the apple in half and give it to your children. That probably would be the ideal thing to do according to these teachings. But your self-importance may get a little freaked out and say, "If I do that, what will *I* have to eat?" At this point, it would be a great practice of lojong not to respect that self-importance, not to take into consideration its continual desire to be met. But you may not be there yet with your practice, and that's all right. If giving the whole apple to your children and enduring some hunger will make you angry and regretful later, then it's probably a better choice to divide it in three. You are giving in to your self-importance, but not as much as if you snuck off and ate the whole apple yourself.

A story about Shariputra, one of the Buddha's closest disciples, illustrates the danger of trying to leap beyond our current level of training. In one of his past lives, Shariputra had taken the bodhisattva vow, the vow to attain enlightenment for the benefit of all beings. To follow this vow, one must train in the practices of letting go of one's self-importance. One day, a Brahmin man asked Shariputra for his right hand. Thinking he was properly following his vow, Shariputra cut the hand off and offered it with his remaining hand. But because Brahmins only use their left hand for certain activities that they consider unclean, the Brahmin became disgusted and said, "How dare you give this to me with your left hand!" Then Shariputra thought, "This bodhisattva path is too difficult!" and temporarily forsook his vow.

It is always suggested that we act in accordance with where we are. We sometimes get inspired, but then we become fearful. This is very common. We have to know how much we are willing to let go and how much we want to hold on. It's not likely that anyone will ask us for a limb. But in many other ways we are called to do more than we are willing to do. How much we are willing to step out of the small self is put to the test every day. So, while respecting our limits, we have to realize that growth will depend on stretching those limits—taking joy in stretching them.

We may not be willing to let go of self-importance because that would mean opening up, softening up, changing our stance. For example, in certain relationships we may act inflexibly because we are holding a grudge. That can lead us to ask abstract questions such as "How could anyone do this practice anyway? It's too difficult, it's impossible, it's outrageous!" But it's not impossible. It all comes down to how much we want to change. Do we really want to practice bodhicitta? Do we really want to escape from the tyranny of our small self? Nobody can force us. Nobody can inspire us if we're unwilling to change. Nothing will happen unless we inspire ourselves.

In our daily life, we have to learn how to work with our limits intelligently and productively. But when we are safely on our meditation cushions, we should feel free to go all the way. Mentally, we can perform any altruistic acts we like as a way of training our minds. We can go back to the apple situation and imagine heroically giving the whole fruit to our children. We can imagine offering our body to a hungry tiger, saying, "Eat me up completely, to your full satisfaction." We can practice lojong in this way, even if in real life we might just throw the tiger the banana in our hand and run away (or even run away *with* the banana).

It's natural for there to be a gap between what we do in real life and what we do on the cushion. But in the safety of our room, we can wholeheartedly drop our care for the small self. When our self-importance comes up, we don't have to cater to it at all. In our minds, we can follow the instructions of the profoundly humorous yogi Geshe Ben, who said, "Whenever the selfish, indulgent mind pops up, I give it a whack on its nose, like one does with a troublesome pig."

Relative Bodhicitta: Post-Meditation

The next three slogans give guidance on how to practice tonglen in "post-meditation," that is, in our daily life, when we aren't sitting on our meditation cushions.

8. Three objects, three poisons, and three roots of virtue.

In order to step out of our small self and develop our altruistic mind, we need to take every opportunity we have to research the qualities of the bodhisattva, especially compassion. Fortunately, our whole life is like a research laboratory. In this lab, there are continual tests, and we ourselves are the perfect research subjects. We are the perfect guinea pigs.

In order to feel compassion, we have to know how others suffer. The only way to learn how others suffer is to learn how we ourselves suffer. So in that way, we can be like guinea pigs for how the world and sentient beings suffer. There is no other way to get this knowledge. I can't go into your mind and experience your suffering directly. I can only know your suffering through inference. And the only reason my inference about another human being's suffering can be accurate is because I am a human being. When I see my own confusions, my own shortcomings, my own attachment and aggression, my own random, disconnected, incoherent, almost schizophrenic mind, what am I seeing? I'm seeing myself as a guinea pig of sentient beings' minds, a guinea pig of beings' ignorance.

If you see your own mind in this way and don't have compassion for yourself, how can you have compassion for others? If you judge yourself as responsible for your ignorance, and therefore guilty and deserving punishment, you probably will see others in the same way. Why would you judge others less harshly than yourself? Do you love them more? Are you more tolerant and forgiving of others? That's probably not true. So it's important first to learn compassion for ourselves and our own confused but innocent mind. When we look in the mirror and see how we create our own turmoil by clinging so hard to this small self, even though it has enslaved us mercilessly through life after life, we can turn that mirror into a window for seeing how others are suffering. Seeing the bigger picture in this way makes it much easier to generate compassion.

Your ongoing disturbing emotions are like a train you want to stop. But the train has been going for too long, it's going too fast, and you, the conductor, are just an infant. In this almost impossible situation, you can spin around with thoughts of "What to do? What to do?

What to do?" Or you can use the power of the emotions themselves and get situated in the heart of compassion for all who are suffering in similar ways. You can practice the exchange of self and other. Think about all those who are going through the same pain as you. Take the cargo of their suffering and load it onto your own boxcars. Make a sincere, heartfelt wish that they won't have to suffer anymore because of your taking on their load. And keep adding boxcars to your train.

This does something wonderful. These days the trains of our confusions and painful emotions are going faster than ever. The modern world as a whole, with its hectic, stimulating lifestyle, has picked up tremendous speed. But even if a train is going a million miles per hour, if you load it with the weight of all beings' suffering, it will stop in an instant. You don't have to push or pull. You don't have to find a more experienced conductor. You don't have to struggle in any way. With such a load, the train will stop naturally, by the laws of physics. All you have to do is get out of your head, situate yourself fully in the heart, and add the suffering of others to your own.

If we really get to know others' afflicted minds by seeing our own, it becomes natural, even joyful, to take on their suffering in this way. Genuine compassion naturally comes with fearlessness. If one person can take care of the needs of many—say, a whole family or a community—that is a cause of joy. If a bodhisattva could take on a dreaded disease such as the Ebola virus and eradicate it permanently from the face of the earth, that would give him or her immense joy. We may not be at that level yet, but that is the attitude we are trying to cultivate here.

Doing research into our own suffering leads to compassion both for ourselves and for others. Our usual habit is to respond first to our own situation, but in this case our priority is to benefit others. So we make the wish that our own suffering be a substitute for everyone else's. We wish that our pain will burn up all the causes of others' pain. Like the Buddha in the hell realm, we think, "Since I have to suffer anyway, why not use my own pain to relieve others having similar pain?" Then we find that acting first on behalf of others actually takes care of our own needs as well. Our goodwill and brave heart directly remedy the root cause of all our suffering, which is our self-importance. Although we're not suppressing our suffering or even wishing it to go away, our compassion alleviates our pain right away, the way a cup of cold water will immediately cool down a pot of boiling water.

If we learn how to do this effectively, we will not only suffer less. We will also stop fearing our own darkness, our own confusion, neurosis, and negativity. Instead of seeing these things as dreadful entities to get rid of, we can learn to embrace them. They provide the ground for our insight into others' suffering, and thus become the seeds of our own compassion. In that way they are our allies, not our enemies. In some Buddhist practices, the instruction is to treat any negativity that arises in our mind the way we would treat a snake in our lap—we throw it out immediately. But lojong is a more sophisticated approach. When we stop rejecting our shadows and darkness, they lose their power over us. We become free of them.

What hinders us most to act freely, live freely, have the freedom to be who we want to be? It is fear, fear of some sort of pain. But if we test ourselves over and over again by practicing tonglen whenever our painful emotions come up, we can become fearless in all circumstances. Without fear, we can confront anything that comes up in life and in death. By taking this approach—not rejecting but embracing our darkness—all our ignorance, confusion, neurosis, and negativity become fertile ground for their opposites to grow. Ignorance is the fertile ground for our awareness to develop. Confusion is the fertile ground for clarity, neurosis the fertile ground for sanity, negativity the fertile ground of positivity. And our self-importance becomes the fertile ground for our bodhicitta to blossom. All we have to do is use our own suffering to stimulate compassion for others, and then take their suffering upon ourselves. When we see what's in our own mind, we're seeing what's in the world's mind as well. If what we see is suffering, that insight becomes compassion for the world. And if what we see in our mind is happiness, we can turn that joy into rejoicing in the good fortune and positive qualities of others.

The slogan refers to "three objects, three poisons, and three roots of virtue." Throughout our lives, we continually encounter objects that we find pleasant, unpleasant, or neutral. Pleasant objects provoke some degree of attachment in our minds. It could be powerful or subtle, but any form of attachment disturbs our mind. Wanting to bring something into our lives or wanting to keep something we already have are emotions based on the small self. Unpleasant objects provoke some degree of aversion or aggression that is unsettling. And our reaction to neutral objects, the ones we don't really notice or those we feel indifferent toward, is related to stupidity. Attachment, aggression, and stupidity are called the "three poisons" because they are the main manifestations of cherishing and protecting the small self. They are like the primary colors of all our other emotions. (When we talk about the *five* poisons, we include arrogance, which is an extension of attachment, and jealousy, an extension of aggression.)

The way to transform these objects and poisons into roots of virtue is by taking on the suffering of others, loading it onto our boxcars. For example, when we are disturbed by aggression, we can think, "At this very moment, so many beings are going through the same painful feeling, or in many cases a much more painful version. May I pile up all of their aggression on myself so that they become free." We can also do this with the discomfort of attachment, the dullness of stupidity, or any other state of mind that we would normally want to reject or suppress.

Instead of burning or burying them, we can use these emotions like manure, which nourishes beautiful plants, helping them blossom with the flowers of bodhicitta. We may grow so affectionate toward our "poisons" that we ask them to linger for a little while in our mind stream. Usually we are in a state of hope or fear regarding these emotions. We hope to be exempt from them, and we fear being stuck with or overwhelmed by them. When we learn how to transform the three objects and poisons into roots of virtue, we go beyond all these hopes and fears. This is a very spacious, joyful mind to have.

9. In all conduct train with maxims.

In his commentary, Jamgon Kongtrul gives a few examples of maxims, such as: "When all the suffering and evil deeds of every sentient being mature in me, may all my virtue and happiness bear fruit in them." In one way or another, all the various slogans and quotations found in the lojong express the mind-set of tonglen. Repeating maxims, especially out loud, is very useful for our lojong practice. Doing so can be scary for our self-importance, which is good! Suffering and the results of evil deeds, for example, are the opposite of what we usually want. Why would we ever ask for them to come to us? The reason is that we are trying to get over the unrelenting hope and fear that cause us always to feel insecure, confined within our small, anxious self. Whether we reject suffering or wish it upon ourselves, if we have created the negative karma that leads to its appearance, that suffering will come. Saying the maxim won't make it happen. But what it will do is whittle away our hope and fear.

A special maxim in the history of the *Seven Points* is: "I offer all gain and victory to others, each and every sentient being. I accept all loss and defeat for myself." Chekawa Yeshe Dorje, the author of the *Seven Points,* first saw these lines in a small text that happened to be sitting on his friend's pillow: *Eight Verses of Training the Mind,* by Geshe Langri Tangpa. Although Chekawa was already an accomplished Buddhist scholar, he found these words so moving that he searched high and low for a teacher who could help him understand them in depth. Eventually he found a teacher named Sharawa, who gave him teachings based on these lines for six years. It is said that this is how Chekawa finally overcame all traces of his self-importance.

The attitude of this maxim is the same as the attitude of the lojong as a whole: one of joy. When we are sitting on a bus and an elderly or handicapped person needs to sit down, we are happy to give up our seat. We gladly take on the slight hardship of standing because of the ease it gives to another. It is important to identify this joyful mind-set when it arises in us, for this is the mind-set of genuinely exchanging self and other.

For the lojong practitioner, altruism is not a show but a delightful experience. We take delight in being kind, compassionate, and generous. When others place their hopes in us—those who are close to us and those who are needy or helpless—we feel honored by their hopes rather than inconvenienced. For example, we feel good about taking care of our pets because they place so much trust in us. It is a delight to be able to help anyone in need: strangers, animals, anyone.

The easiest, most convenient, most self-serving life is not the best one for our mind training. Doing difficult things for others, especially when there is no profit for *me,* helps balance out our life and break the habit of our self-serving attitude. We can stretch ourselves in ways that may seem foolish from the conventional point of view but in terms of lojong are not. The "loss" we usually fear can bring us much more joy than "gain." If you've never learned how to be joyful when you lose, the first time you take delight in loss is a revelation. If you've always had the habit of having and never not having, the first time you take delight in someone else having instead of you is an experience to cherish.

There are so many ways we can acquire wisdom and learn new things in life. As lojong practitioners we should be keen to learn, rather than thinking we already know. And when we learn, we can share our knowledge with others who want to listen. But if another person isn't open and wants to teach you something, then instead of competing to be the teacher, it's better to be open to what the other person has to say. If they want to pass on to you what they know, give them that satisfaction. If a child wants to teach you how to fix a toy, give the child that pleasure. It doesn't cost you anything. Depending on what the other person wants, you can be happy either as a teacher or a student. As long as altruism, and not self-importance, is your guide, you will always be practicing mind training. As long as you are cherishing the happiness of others, practices such as tonglen will be full of joy.

When we memorize and recite these maxims, such as the one about gain and loss, we may at first feel like a parrot. That is a fine beginning, as we are still just learning to step out of the small self. Over time our understanding of the words will deepen. In this case, we will come to understand that "all sentient beings" are not really "other." Since bodhisattvas deeply understand that all beings are no different at the core, and that identifying with this "self" is an arbitrary mental habit, they are not sacrificing anything by giving their gain and victory to "others." A father who teaches his son how to play a sport will gladly let the child win because he considers his son to be a part of himself. The bodhisattva has a similar attitude, but vastly expanded to include all sentient beings.

As our understanding of these maxims deepens, we will see more clearly how reciting and contemplating them transforms our experience. When we can say them with conviction based on clear reasoning and sound emotional intelligence, we will feel tremendous relief and inner strength. Then it won't matter if we experience victory or defeat because we'll have achieved the much greater victory of overcoming our self-importance.

10. Begin the sequence of taking with oneself.

When we are first introduced to the practice of tonglen, it may be difficult to imagine taking on the suffering of others. Our clinging to the small self may be too strong, and working with the duality of self and other may be too painful. If that is the case, we can ease into the main practice by practicing tonglen with our future self. This is a gradual way of bridging the gap between self and other.

If you take out a thirty-year mortgage on your house, you will eventually pay a lot of interest. So if you find yourself with the means to pay it off more quickly, that is a wise choice. You will be free from your burden sooner, and you will end up paying less money. This reasoning also applies to our negative karma. Right now our mind is in relatively good shape. We have favorable conditions, especially since we have been introduced to the wisdom and skillful means of lojong. The results of our past negative deeds are sure to appear in the future, and who knows what shape we'll be in then? Reaping our karmic fruit during future unfavorable circumstances is like paying off our mortgage with lots of compounded interest. So, while we have the chance, why not take on the suffering of our future self?

Thinking that this future self is "me" is really just another arbitrary clinging to what we are habituated to. In fact, in the future our self will have changed from our present self in every way. Every body part will have transformed, subtly or grossly; every aspect of our personality will have shifted, subtly or grossly; and every perception, thought, and feeling of our future self will be arising for the first time. A continuity joins these selves, but there is nothing that stays the same, not within this lifetime, and obviously not as we evolve through future lives. Even tomorrow's self will be different from today's.

In this way, taking on the suffering of our future self is essentially no different from taking on the suffering of "others." But for some people, using this method to begin one's tonglen practice can be an effective bridge to the versions described in the previous slogans.

Transforming Adversity into the Path of Enlightenment

11. When the world is full of evil, transform misfortune into the path of awakening.

Many of us tend to feel like victims in our lives. I know that I do! We may feel victimized by other people, by our bad luck, by evil spirits, or by "the system." But whatever we blame, the experience is similar. We feel deeply hurt and helpless, which can make us frustrated, angry, and jealous. In such a state, we can't be productive in worldly life. All our time is taken up with these emotions. And of course, as victims we can't be productive in our spiritual life. So life in general becomes unproductive as our victimhood makes us withdraw into our pain. So the question is, how do we summon the courage to live productively when faced with adverse circumstances?

First of all, it helps to know that there may be more going on in our situation than meets the eye. We may be at a plateau in our spiritual path, not progressing because nothing is really challenging us. We may be stalling and getting lethargic. In times like these, difficult and painful situations often arise to incite us, to test how much we have overcome our attachment to a small self. Furthermore, it is said that those who have come onto the bodhisattva's path, who are devoting much of their time and energy to attaining enlightenment for the benefit of others, could possibly face more suffering in this life than they ordinarily would. Because of our aspirations to purify our self-importance sooner than later, the karmic seeds from our negative past deeds bear fruit more quickly. If we ignore these possibilities and just think of ourselves as victims, we will miss great opportunities to go forward on the path.

Difficult times, for ourselves and for the world as a whole, give us the ideal conditions for practicing tonglen. Say you are doing what you would really like to do, perhaps lying in a deck chair on the beach, beholding the shimmering blue Mediterranean Sea. The glorious sun is shining and a cabana boy has just brought you your favorite drink with one of those little umbrellas. Go ahead, try practicing tonglen in that situation.

At this moment, you may be far, far away from that sunny beach and that little umbrella. You may be facing the darkness of your mind: fear, confusion, a contracted state of being. You may be at your wit's end. But now you have this incredible opportunity to practice the exchange of self and other. And in these circumstances, tonglen has a lot more power to purify our self-importance than it does on the deck chair. Since self-importance is the true cause of all our pain, we can take delight in this chance to sow seeds for future happiness. And that happiness will be far more fulfilling than the fleeting pleasure of being on a vacation. Happiness based on pure, ever-flowing love and care for others is the deepest, most stable form of happiness there is. So instead of feeling like victims, we can take charge of our minds and move in that direction.

This slogan is an introduction to the basic attitude of *Point Three,* "Transforming Adversity into the Path of Enlightenment." The slogans that follow show us in more detail the relative and absolute methods for carrying out this attitude.

Relative Bodhicitta

12. Realize all faults spring from one source.

Our lives are made of countless events, involving infinite causes and conditions that flow from past to present to future. In order to make sense of so much information, we tend to simplify complex events into stories: "So and so did this to me. Such and such happened to me. As a result I'm this way and am behaving like this." When we feel like a victim, we have a story about who or what is causing us to suffer. We see how a person or a situation is bringing us suffering from the outside, and that is where we place all the blame. When we're entrenched in our victimhood and want to justify our feelings, we feel we know the story, the whole story, behind it. We don't even think this is a story. But is our interpretation of events accurate? Or is there a more truthful and helpful way of looking at things?

One of the functions of the lojong slogans is that they help us discriminate among our stories. They teach us how to think about our lives in both the most honest and most favorable ways. Stories are helpful to us when they are in line with how things naturally function in the world—with the laws of cause and effect. Such stories lead us to greater harmony and happiness. Unhelpful stories merely perpetuate our confusion.

The idea of victimhood is one of the most unhelpful stories. But unless we are open and inspired to see things another way, we can't practice this slogan. What compounds our problem here is that when we feel bad about ourselves, when we feel victimized, or even when we're just having a bad hair day, we tend to feel less interested in looking into the truth. This is a sign of not really being ready to get over our suffering. If we are truly inspired to transform our mind, to go from victim to bodhisattva, the only way is to be open to a new story.

Here is a more truthful story that will start to lead us out of our suffering. All the suffering that we and others experience, that every being in the whole world experiences, comes from one source: clinging to this small self. Every suffering has come from self-importance gone out of control, leading to attachment, aggression, jealousy, arrogance, and stupidity, which in turn have led to all the actions of body, speech, and mind that have harmed others. And the results of this harm we've inflicted on others have come back to us as the difficult situations we face in this life.

Less ego equals more peace. More ego equals more tension. The harmony of every relationship in the world, whether between countries, between religions, within communities, or within families, depends on whether there is more or less ego. Less ego means understanding each other's experiences better, being able to step into each others' shoes. More ego means more self-absorption, more undermining each other with negativity. Our self-importance is the source of all our interpersonal problems. It increases our jealousy, our competitiveness, our arrogance. It makes us pushy, demanding, grasping, hard to please, hard to get along with, hard to communicate with. We're not satisfied with an equal share; we want more of everything than anyone else.

Ego and its attendant emotions are contagious. But however you catch the flu, you end up with the same symptoms. You may not start off very attached. But if you spend a lot of time with someone who is attached, sooner or later you may feel the need to become attached, for the sake of self-protection. Similarly, if you're not aggressive but spend a lot of time with someone who is, you may naturally feel drawn into a more aggressive mind-set as a means of self-defense. This natural result of interdependence causes tension to build within relationships. You may feel like you don't always need to get your way. But if you're with someone very demanding, you start to think, "Why am I always surrendering to this person's demands? Am I totally spineless? What about *my* needs?" In this way, self-importance sets up walls between people.

To reduce our ego, we need to contemplate how it is the cause of all these problems. We need to be inspired to look into our own experience, both of suffering and of causing others to suffer. We need to examine this from all angles and see the truth of this slogan. We don't have to be able to remember our past lives and trace all our misfortunes to remote times. Just in this life, we have mountains of evidence about how our self-importance has led to our own and others' suffering. But when we feel like a victim, when we're in that state of helplessness and frustration, it takes a lot of strength to put the blame on our own mental habit of cherishing the small self. We have to go through many layers of resistance to get deep into our heart and acknowledge the true cause of our suffering. Sometimes we summon up our courage to penetrate these layers, but after getting through one or two, we give up. We start to make excuses and go off on tangents. We think, "I've practiced enough today. I'm done." And then we can easily get back into feeling like a victim.

It takes mindfulness to keep penetrating these layers, and to realize, as we get deeper and deeper, that we are already feeling some relief from our victimhood. We are not blaming outer people and circumstances as much, and that feels good. What happens when we get down to our raw attachment to the self and admit that it is the sole cause of our suffering? Again, we have the practice of tonglen. We take on the suffering of all who are plagued by self-importance, so that they may be free of it. We load it onto our boxcars. This brings about a deep shift within, and we feel released. Our self-clinging, the cause of all our suffering, has become transformed into a source of increasing care for others. We feel so enriched that we almost want more suffering and even more ego!

Our intention in practicing tonglen, however, should not be merely to alleviate our own pain. If we aren't mindful of such a motivation, our self-centeredness can sneak in and hijack our practice. This self who wants to be healed can be tricky, so we need to be wary of it. Healing can only come about by decreasing our self-centeredness. Instead of making our pain or misfortune go away, this process works against our habitual reactions to those things. It works against our wanting them to go away so badly. It works against our rejection of difficult experiences, which is an action we take to protect our small self.

Lojong isn't just a trick, a twist of psychology. It is based on empirical evidence: knowing where suffering and happiness come from. We aren't trying to fool ourselves here. When we feel relief from our self-importance and realize that it has always been our only problem, we challenge our habit of unquestioning loyalty to this small self. For the first time, we see with our own eyes that this self may not deserve our blind and unconditional protection and cherishing.

Shantideva says to his self-importance: "You have caused me suffering for hundreds of lives in samsara. Now I remember all my grudges and will destroy you, my own evil mind." This is not just an emotional outburst coming from frustration. Great bodhisattvas such as Shantideva have arrived at their altruistic mind-set by filing an intelligent case against self-centered attachment. They have examined the subject thoroughly and come up with solid reasons for not clinging to the small self. Having seen what binds them to perpetual suffering, they are able to overcome that ignorance and become free of the cycle of samsara.

I feel that applying our intelligence in this way is especially important for practitioners in the West, where people really like to think things through. The key is discerning between our true foe, self-importance, and our true friend, bodhicitta. With such discernment, we can see clearly, for the first time, the source of all our troubles. Then we are like a soldier fighting in a war who suddenly realizes his king is a crook. Without a second thought, the soldier's inspiration to be loyal and risk his life for this cause automatically falls away.

13. Meditate upon gratitude toward all.

When things go wrong in our lives, we tend to place all the blame on something outside ourselves, which only compounds our root problem of self-importance. "Realize all faults spring from one source" is the antidote to that confused and unhelpful mentality. "Meditate upon gratitude toward all" works with another distorted way of looking at things. This slogan and the problem it addresses are the mirror image of the previous one.

We tend to think that everything good in our life comes to us because we deserve it, either thanks to our efforts or simply because of who we are. We're entitled to our good fortune. Good things are meant to happen to us. That's just the way things should be. But this attitude has nothing to do with reality. Our being and all the circumstances in our life are deeply interconnected with others. Anything that happens to us, good or bad, comes about because of that interconnection.

Everything positive in our lives has been a gift from other sentient beings. This is what we need to meditate upon until it is clear in our mind. First of all, without others being involved in your life, you wouldn't even be here. You have a body that you generally identify with. You say things like "I go" and "I sit." But this body was just an egg and a sperm that your parents donated to you, giving you a place for your consciousness to enter. It's not inherently yours; it's just a borrowed home. Another woman and another man, your so-called parents, gave you the gift of this seed, and all the body parts and functions that developed from it were the result of that gift. Before receiving the gift, you had nothing. There was just a homeless consciousness being driven helplessly by karma.

After conception, this kind woman, now known as your "mother," gave you a place in which to survive and grow. She fed you with her own food. She never asked for rent. And when you were ready to be born, she went through so much pain to bring you out into the world. Then, once you were out of the womb, you wouldn't have survived for even a few hours if you'd been left alone. But this woman held you to her body, kept you warm with her heat, and fed you with her milk. And from then on she did everything for you. At every moment, she was concerned about your well-being. Without the love and affection of your parents, you wouldn't have developed into a functioning adult. If your parents and teachers hadn't taught you, you wouldn't even be able to say the most basic words, like *house* or *table*. You would have no way of communicating with the world.

By contemplating further along these lines, we can see that everything we have, everything we think of as "me" or "mine," is actually the gift of others. All the parts of our body and brain; all our possessions, food, clothing, shelter; all our knowledge, wisdom, skill, personality traits, talents, morals, ethics, positive intentions—everything is the gift of others. Without others, we would have nothing. We wouldn't even be able to think or feel. We can't take any of this for granted. Let's not think this has all appeared for us spontaneously. That would be a false story, based on self-importance and delusion. Everything in our lives comes from the kindness of others.

This is not only true in our ordinary, conventional life; it's also true in terms of our path of awakening. We will only go beyond our confusion and become fully at ease with our lives if we receive the kindness of others. Our innermost enlightened nature is free from all flaws and rich with wisdom, compassion, and the power to benefit others. But without buddhas, bodhisattvas, and our teachers, we would have no hope of realizing this enlightened nature. We wouldn't even have an inkling that we have such a nature to realize.

You may think, "But doesn't all my good fortune come from my merit, the results of my own positive actions in the past?" Yes, that's true. But where did that merit come from? It came from others. Your health, attractiveness, and good physique are the results of your patience in past lives. But without others to irritate you, how could you have practiced patience? Your wealth came from your past generosity, which required others to be poor. Your fortunate human birth came from doing positive deeds and avoiding negativity in relation to others. Without others, there is no way to accumulate merit.

Our ability to progress along the path and our prospect of enlightenment depend on cultivating bodhicitta. In order to do that, we need to develop love and compassion, which requires other sentient beings. We need to practice the exchange of self and other. We rely on enlightened beings as guides on the path. But in order to *do* this path, we need our fellow sentient beings. Therefore, buddhas and sentient beings are equal in terms of how much they help us.

Also, if we care about pleasing enlightened beings, we have to serve sentient beings, because the welfare of beings is their greatest concern. When we harm beings, we're also hurting the buddhas and bodhisattvas. Because we feel deep respect and appreciation, we may wish to make offerings to the enlightened ones. But since they have gone beyond all attachment, the most welcome offering we can make to buddhas is to benefit sentient beings. We could offer an entire world full of gold to the buddhas, but they would be more touched if we offered a handful of coins to a homeless person. As Shantideva says, we shouldn't see sentient beings merely as sentient beings. We should see them as the cause of our enlightenment.

Even after attaining enlightenment, you still need the presence of sentient beings. Without them, enlightenment would be very boring. What would you do? With all your understanding, your compassion, and your ability to work skillfully with others, what would you do without sentient beings? Most of the point of becoming enlightened would be gone. So even once you're enlightened, no one is kinder than sentient beings.

We should contemplate sentient beings in these ways and develop genuine gratitude and love for them, never forgetting that we're walking the path to enlightenment in order to free them from suffering. Our expressions of gratitude should be more than eloquent words spoken without feeling. To say "I appreciate this, I'm grateful for that, thank you for this, thank you for that" without any feeling is just hypocrisy. So we have to work on stripping away this hypocrisy until we really start to feel things in the heart. The great masters have so much care in their hearts that they can give anything, even their very lives, to others without hesitation.

Meditating upon being grateful to everyone also radically alters our ideas of what is helpful and harmful in our lives. For those who have been obviously helpful, such as our parents, we develop greater appreciation. We stop taking credit for everything positive that has happened to us. This lessens our self-importance, which is the main point of practicing lojong. But if liberating ourselves from the prison of ego-clinging is important to us, then the so-called harm doers in our lives may help us even more.

In the nineteenth century, the enlightened teacher and wandering yogi Patrul Rinpoche traveled all over eastern Tibet, spreading Shantideva's teachings far and wide. One of his favorite sayings was that the outcome of suffering is better than the outcome of happiness. In happy times, we become forgetful and indulge more in our self-centered emotions. But in painful times, we develop renunciation toward suffering and its causes and conditions. We appreciate the spiritual path and our opportunity to work with our mind internally. Therefore Patrul Rinpoche's preference was for suffering. The irony is that for people like him who have completely rid their minds of self-importance, suffering doesn't occur even when it's wished for! But for people like us, other beings will continue to bring us harm, and as lojong practitioners we can make good use of it.

We can start by changing the habitual story of harm to a more helpful one. Rather than lament all the harm that beings are doing to us, we should consider all the harm we've done to them. The only reason these beings are harming us now is because of what we've done to them in the past. It's a simple boomerang effect. When you throw a boomerang, it comes back to you, not to someone else, right? And not only have we harmed them in the past, we're still causing them harm by inciting their negativity. Everything they do to hurt us creates negative karma, which will bring them suffering in the future. Following this improved story enables us to convert resentment into compassion.

We can also reflect on how our relationships with these harm doers have been entirely different in the past. In past lives, every one of them has been a parent to us. Every one has loved us, cherished us, delivered us so much joy, protected us from so much pain. The intensity of our present experience blinds us to these truths, but when we take the time to contemplate, we can see things in this more productive way. We should contemplate these beings' past kindness to us until we feel so much affection that we could swallow them up and bring them into our hearts.

Once we've cultivated love and compassion for our "enemies," we should practice tonglen. This pacifies much of the tension that both parties feel. If you consider someone an enemy, they will consider you an enemy, and treat you as such. If you consider someone a friend, they will consider you a friend. If you consider someone to be your mother, they will consider you to be their child. This is how karma and interdependence work. When the Buddha was about to attain enlightenment under the bodhi tree, the demonic forces known as *maras* came and threw weapons at him. These didn't distract the Buddha; through the power of his compassion, he turned the weapons into flowers. When Gandhi used nonviolence to achieve independence, even most of the British people eventually supported him. There are similar stories about Martin Luther King Jr., Nelson Mandela, and His Holiness the Dalai Lama.

Being grateful to our "enemies" and practicing tonglen go against our habits. In our daily interactions with others, we have to be continually alert to our tendencies. But if we do give way to habit, we should look at ourselves honestly and confess our mistake. Until our minds are completely transformed, we will keep falling down. The choice is between getting up and starting to walk again or giving up and staying on the ground. If we keep lying down, nothing will result but greater depression and hopelessness. As Shantideva says, a powerful cobra can't be harmed by large birds of prey, but if it's lying on the ground as if dead, even crows will peck at it.

The antidote to such low self-esteem, as Shantideva suggests, is to bring forth a sense of positive, courageous pride. This pride, though it may have a tinge of self-importance, works effectively against our neurosis. After we have remedied our low self-esteem, we can then transcend our pride as well.

We can develop this courage by practicing tonglen, and especially by focusing on subjects that bring up strong clinging to the self. For example, we can think about illnesses that we find especially repulsive, filling us with fear and disgust. If we imagine taking these illnesses from others and bringing them into our heart, that will help lessen the self-grasping. We often think of our body as "me," so focusing on the body in this way is powerful. Don't worry—it won't actually make you get the disease. All it will do is make you stronger and stronger in your practice of bodhicitta.

We have so many phobias about illnesses and other forms of suffering. Phobias are a weakness of the mind, brought about by our self-importance. If we genuinely do tonglen with all the diseases and other situations that horrify us—the very things whose names we can barely mention—it will frighten our self-centered mind. Why would we want to do this to ourselves? By deliberately frightening our ego, we bring it closer to the surface, exposing our own weakness. Ordinarily we hope and believe that protecting our small self will keep us from suffering. We can only overcome this misconception by shedding light on it with the practices of mind training.

Great practitioners like Shantideva and Patrul Rinpoche have this mental attitude toward troublemakers: "Come here and take everything away from me! If you want my flesh, go ahead and take it! If you want my blood, you can have it! If you want my bones, my skin, my organs, I give them to you gladly! Relax and enjoy the feast!" They see the arrival of harm doers in their lives as a chance to purify past negative karma. Since these acts need to reckoned with one way or another, this harm speeds up our process of purification. This is a tremendously courageous attitude, but if we are interested in letting go of the attachments that imprison us, there is nothing better. Confronting our negative karma head on is a highly evolved practice of patience. Patience is much more than putting up with irritations. When intentionally cultivated in this way, it becomes a source of incredible power and confidence.

Every Buddhist teaching we read or listen to is ultimately about getting liberated. The path of liberation is to abandon grasping to the self and to cherish sentient beings. If you aren't understanding this in the teachings, then you are probably misunderstanding something. We can look at our spiritual path as a battle between our selfish mind and our altruistic mind. Since our selfish mind is the greatest enemy of our own and others' happiness, we want to do everything possible for the altruistic side to win. We need to keep the enemy always under scrutiny. We need to disempower it with our wisdom and skillful means, exposing its faults and reprimanding it. At the same time, we need to boost our altruistic mind by increasing and deepening any thoughts and emotions that are in line with bodhicitta.

Patrul Rinpoche tells the story of a Brahmin who kept track of his mind by using two piles of pebbles. For every positive thought he would add a white pebble to one pile, and for every negative thought he would add a black pebble to another pile. In the beginning, the black pile was much bigger than the white pile, but as he kept observing his mind, the white pile got bigger and bigger in relation to the black one. Eventually he stopped adding black pebbles altogether. This transformation came about through his power of observation, along with his understanding of the effects of altruism and selfishness.

Since everything that happens in our lives is our mind's experience, if we train our flexible mind with such methods, it will get used to positive actions and naturally transform itself. When our mind is left alone to follow its habits and manifest its neurosis, it tends to be more selfish and unreasonable than the most spoiled brat. As Geshe Ben said, "There's nothing else on my daily schedule than to be alert to the devil of self-importance inside me. When it wakes up, I have to wake up. When it is asleep, I can also be at rest." Meditating on gratitude is one of the best practices available for getting our mind used to focusing on others and reducing our clinging to the small self.

"Realize all faults spring from one source" and "Meditate upon being grateful to everyone" show the relative ways of turning difficult situations to our advantage. Jesus advised his disciples to "turn the other cheek." A more modern saying goes, "Never let a good crisis go to waste." Our resilience and our ability to rebound strictly depend on how we work with crisis. Every time we face difficult circumstances, we have a chance to increase our bodhicitta and purify much of the negativity we have created in the past.

Absolute Bodhicitta

14. Meditate upon illusory appearance as the four kayas.
This is the unsurpassable protection of emptiness.

As I said in the commentary for *Point Two,* absolute bodhicitta refers to direct insight into the empty nature of all phenomena. To call something "empty" does not mean it doesn't appear or function. Emptiness is not a nihilistic void. The emptiness teachings only say that we can't grasp or pin anything down—not the outer world, not our "self," not even our own mind.

Practitioners who have realized the absolute truth of emptiness have the ultimate antidote to difficult situations. Confident that all phenomena are nothing but a dream, and knowing their own ungraspable minds to be indestructible, they realize no harm can truly be done to them. All "harm" is illusion. When adversity does arise in their lives, they are happy for the chance to test their confidence. For this reason, they regard all harmful beings and situations as their teachers.

Most of us, however, are not there yet. As Jamgon Kongtrul states in his commentary, "Authentic absolute bodhicitta will not arise in the mind streams of beginners. But relative bodhicitta, should they train in it, will surely be born." Relative practices such as gratitude are like narrow, winding country roads. The absolute view of emptiness is like the highway. If we have a genuine experience of connecting to the absolute, it is very powerful and efficient.

But if we misunderstand emptiness, we may be fooling ourselves. We may imagine that we're traveling on the highway, but this may be a daydream, and the fact is we're not getting anywhere. So it's important to use our critical intelligence here. The country road is much more grounded and tangible. We can feel every bump and turn. And eventually, when we are ready, it leads to the highway. Jamgon Kongtrul continues: "With the development of relative bodhicitta, absolute bodhicitta is naturally realized." So with this caveat, I will go into the slogan.

When we examine our minds we find that we are constantly protecting ourselves from threats. Inanimate objects and circumstances threaten us, and sometimes people seem to wish us harm. Sometimes threats come from outside us, other times they appear to come from within. But all of these appearances are nothing but our own mind's projections and elaborations. This slogan is about developing a firm conviction that all these threatening phenomena are actually delusions.

Even though threatening phenomena appear vividly to our perceptions, when we investigate closely we can find no moment when they truly exist or have time to cause us any harm. This book seems to stay the same from moment to moment, but that is just our mind's conception. Every instant, every particle of this book is changing. We can't see this change at a subtle level, but we can know it through our understanding. If these subtle changes didn't happen, then how could this same book, years from now, appear "old"? If an image of this book appeared in a movie or on our computer screen, that image would be made of many flashes of light per second. In reality, each instant there is a subtly different book, a new book that only resembles the ones before and after it.

This is true for all things. Just as something arises, it immediately disappears. Threatening phenomena are mind's delusion because nothing lasts long enough to be a threat. When we examine what appears to be a threat, we can't say anything definite about it. How could we say anything definite about something that changes every instant? When we talk about this book, which instant's book are we talking about? The past is gone, the future has not arrived, and the present moment dissolves as soon as it arises, so there is nothing to pinpoint.

By contemplating this reasoning for a long time, we can eventually see there are really no phenomena "out there." Everything that appears is simply the product of mind's awareness. It is no more tangible than space. This includes what we take to be our body and mind—all the components that we take to be our "self." We ourselves are no more tangible than space. This self is nothing but the product of mind's awareness. How can anything threaten space? How can awareness that is like space be harmed? Whatever we perceive as a threat is also made from spacelike awareness. How can space threaten space? If we divide space into "eastern space" and "western space," can either of these threaten the other?

In this way, we can eventually understand that all the experiences we go through are dreamlike delusions. Your self, and the threats you perceive—such as illnesses and their so-called causes—are nothing but thoughts. If we try to pinpoint our thoughts or find any characteristics in them, we can't find anything. Our thoughts are empty of any reality. These empty thoughts lead to emotions, which also seem tangible. But again, when we look closely at our emotions, we can't find anything to put our finger on. Therefore our mind, which most of the time feels burdened and bewildered by thoughts and emotions, is ultimately free of them. Just like the mind of the buddhas—and the mind of all sentient beings, for that matter—our absolute mind can't be affected by any thoughts, obstacle makers, or diseases. It is like the blue sky, which can't be affected by any clouds that arise within it.

In order to experience the spacelike nature of our mind, we need to let it be. If we have a jar of muddy water, the easiest way to make it clear is to let the mud and sediment settle to the bottom. Instead of stirring it up, we let the water clarify itself. Our disturbing thoughts and emotions aren't worthy of so much fascinated attention. If we take them too seriously, we only stir them up more. We can simply forget about them and rest in our spacelike awareness. Our thoughts and emotions are also nothing but space. They can't tie us up in knots. They can only harm us if we solidify them ourselves, with our misunderstanding. Can space be tied into knots? Can you tie yourself up with a rope made from the hair of a turtle? Of course not. These things are impossible. So if we realize that our thoughts and everything they pertain to are as insubstantial as space and as unfindable as turtle's hair, what harm can they do us?

The teaching on the "four kayas" is a way of talking about this subject from an enlightened being's point of view. The four kayas are aspects of our mind's experience. As we have seen, our mind and all phenomena are like space, empty of any characteristics that we can pinpoint. The Sanskrit word for this emptiness aspect is *dharmakaya*. The empty dharmakaya is the nature of all things. But this emptiness is not a void: appearances manifest out of it. This manifestation is known as the *nirmanakaya*. We can think of the empty nature as a movie screen and the appearance that manifests on it as light from a film projector. There is no way to separate the projected appearance from the screen. Similarly, emptiness and appearance are always together. They are like two sides of a coin: whatever appears is empty, and whatever is empty appears. This inseparability aspect is called the *sambhogakaya*. Finally, though we use these words to distinguish aspects in language, from the awakened point of view, the mind doesn't have three distinct natures. In reality, all the kayas are just one experience of mind. This aspect of union is called the *svabhavikakaya*.

A thorough explanation of the four kayas is beyond the scope of this book. The essence of this instruction is that if you can rest your mind in its absolute nature, following this slogan or the previous slogans on absolute bodhicitta, there is no better way to work with whatever threatens you. Yet it is not so easy, when our minds are so habituated to viewing all appearances as real. Therefore, we should always work with the relative methods as well.

Special Practices

15. The four practices are the best of means.

In addition to the relative and absolute practices mentioned above, there are four special practices that we can use to work with our difficult situations. The first practice is *accumulating merit*. As we have seen in *Point One,* "First, train in the preliminaries," we accumulate merit through any actions that are in line with bodhicitta, the wish to attain enlightenment for the benefit of all sentient beings. Through the law of cause and effect, positive deeds bring about happiness. This is a simple, straightforward approach to dealing with difficulties. When misfortune befalls us, we recognize that it is the result of our own negative actions based on self-importance. This motivates us to accumulate merit by focusing on others. If we trust the operation of karma and consciously sow the seeds of happiness, then we can see our current misfortunes as temporary, and therefore less threatening. This will make us feel less stuck, more optimistic.

Any practice oriented toward becoming enlightened for the sake of others generates tremendous merit. Making offerings, reciting mantras, traveling to holy sites, releasing lives, giving aid to the poor, serving the community of fellow practitioners, and contemplating the illusory nature of phenomena are among the traditional Buddhist practices for accumulating merit. But in his commentary, Jamgon Kongtrul highlights one method that goes particularly well with the attitude of fearlessness we try to cultivate through lojong. This is to "make supplications to cease all your hopes and fears."

We should think and adopt the attitude:

If I am to suffer, bless me to suffer, so that I may learn whatever I need to learn through suffering. If it's good for me to be sick, bless me to be sick. I may only have to endure this illness for a short time, so may I benefit from it while I can. May this illness keep me from being so caught up in the superficial glitter of life and help me develop renunciation to self-importance. May it help me understand more deeply the teachings of dharma.

If I am to get well, may I get well and make the best use of my health to cultivate altruism. If I am to die, may I die in peace, with my heart full of bodhicitta. To die now with bodhicitta is much better than to live for a long time and accumulate negative deeds. Either way, until I die, may I train in bodhicitta and aspire to continue this path into my next life.

Bless me to experience now whatever will purify my negative karma and the causes of future suffering. Bless me to experience whatever will

purify my self-centered mind-set, the source of all my hopes and fears.
Whatever happens to me, may I use it to understand better how other
beings are suffering and to increase my motivation to take their pain upon
myself. May I use any misfortune as fodder for my practice of exchanging
self and other.

In short, we can accumulate a lot of merit by having a spirit of trust
and surrender. This is a more open and courageous attitude than our
predictable, programmed reactions of self-pity and despair. If there's a
cure, why worry? If there's not a cure, again, why worry? There is something outrageous about this simple approach to our suffering, but it
leads to our becoming carefree, released from the bondage of our own
self-attachments.

Compared to the external sufferings of illness and so on, the sufferings of hope and fear are far more complex and persistent, creating a
shakiness within. For example, when you are depressed, you automatically have such a powerful desire to feel better. You feel this desire for
relief in your whole body. Getting rid of your pain is your most urgent
priority. But this desperation is exactly what makes the depression dig
in its heels. If you can approach your suffering by tackling the very
mechanism of hope and fear—and its root, self-importance—then
this impossible depression starts to feel less solid. When we don't battle against it, the painful, disturbing sensation in our chest can begin
to melt away.

The second special practice is *confessing* our negative, self-centered
actions. But before confessing, we should first use our critical intelligence to connect the dots of cause and effect leading to our current
adversity. This is the connection between our present suffering and
acts perpetrated by our small self. Whether we can remember them
or they occurred during a past life, these acts are responsible for our
current circumstances. Understanding this, we can develop regret. But
it is crucial here not to confuse healthy regret with guilt.

Regret is based on honest, objective self-reflection. We acknowledge that our own mind has sown the seeds of our present difficulties, but with the attitude that these seeds are purifiable. If possible, we retrace our steps and see how our confusion and self-centered attachment led to our mistakes. We examine the chain of events objectively, scientifically. We value whatever information we glean, and use it to change for the better. We can regret our actions based on self-importance, but there is no reason to feel bad about them. We have the same unfortunate but innocent habit as every other sentient being. It doesn't come from any intrinsic badness or original sin. It comes from ignorance, removable ignorance.

Guilt, on the other hand, is counterproductive. When we identify with a solid, intrinsic self, we feel so guilty that we can't bear to examine what we have done. Guilt is a mind-set that dwells on the inability to accept what has happened. Rather than regret our past mistakes and accept that they came from our ignorant, confused mind, we painfully solidify the whole event by overchewing our shame. "How could *I*, who have this fixed, unchangeable character, be so *bad*? It can't be true—I can't bear to look!" Guilt is the opposite of critical intelligence; it is really extra-strength ego. But that doesn't mean you should feel guilty about your guilt!

Next, armed with positive, productive regret, we resolve to do our best not to give in to the demands of our small self. We can't immediately halt our habit of self-clinging, once and for all, but we can form a strong intention to keep counteracting it until our care for others becomes greater than our care for ourself. Once we make this resolution firmly in our minds, we then reverse our habits by continually increasing our bodhicitta with practices such as exchanging self and other.

The method of purifying our negativity through critical intelligence and confession becomes even more effective when we invoke the support of the buddhas and bodhisattvas. By asking them to witness our practice and to guide and bless us, we connect ourselves to our own bodhicitta. These enlightened beings are not external figures who are intrinsically superior to us. They are embodiments of our own enlightened nature, which becomes more and more apparent as we let go of our clinging to the small self. We may imagine that enlightened beings who support us are somewhere outside, but in fact they are inseparable from the essence of our own mind.

When we confess our wrongdoing to enlightened beings, they are beyond judgments. Since they already know what we have done and see everything as a product of mental confusion and ignorance, we can feel open to confess, without fear of their judgment or contempt. The practice of confession is getting ourselves to the point of courage to cleanse our mind. The enlightened beings serve as witnesses to this process.

The one good quality of negativity is that it can be purified. Although it temporarily disconnects us from our own altruistic nature, it is not intrinsic. It is no more substantial than the steam that covers a mirror when we breathe on it. By engaging in the practice of confession, we can wipe off this thin layer of steam and allow the brilliance and clarity of our compassionate mirror-like mind to shine forth.

The third special practice is *offering tormas to gods and demons.* Tormas are a kind of offering cake, which in Tibet are usually made from barley flour. In the West, we can offer cookies. In his commentary, Jamgon Kongtrul says little about the tormas themselves, instead emphasizing the attitude behind this offering, especially when offering to the "demons," who can be seen as anyone, visible or not, who brings us trouble. He encourages us to have the fearless attitude of asking the demons to bring us even *more* trouble, so that we can repay all our karmic debts and destroy our habit of clinging to a small self. On top of that, we ask for the sufferings of all beings to pile up on ourselves, so that they may all be free.

This is much like what Jesus did on the cross. For me Jesus shows what it means to take the spirit of tonglen to the highest level. His aspiration to exchange self and other inspired countless people across the globe and resulted in Christianity becoming the most popular religion in history. Right now we probably can't practice tonglen at such a high level, but we can gradually train our minds in that direction. If we feel it's too much for us to ask the demons to bring us more trouble, we can at least try to generate love and care for them, and let them know that they are included in our practice of bodhicitta.

Finally, there is the special practice of *offering tormas to the dakinis and protectors*. These are powerful beings who have committed themselves to help sincere practitioners attain enlightenment. We can think of the dakinis and protectors as members of our spiritual community, as companions on our bodhisattva's path. Many of us have the "cowboy mentality" of refusing to ask for help because we think we don't need it. This attitude can be full of pride and arrogance. It doesn't acknowledge how the world actually works, through the play of interdependence. If your plumbing breaks, you may not be able to fix it yourself. Would you be too proud to call a plumber and instead sit there scratching your head for days? Even more so than a good plumber, dakinis and protectors have tremendous skills and power, which can help us along the path. They have taken on the responsibility of being guardians of dharma practitioners, so if we offer them tormas and ask for their help, they can do things that are truly wondrous.

16. Use whatever you face as a practice immediately.

We may judge whatever comes into our lives as "good" or "bad," but both good and bad have equal potential to make us confused. How to deal with adversity has been the main subject of the last few slogans. But even when good things happen, we still often react in ways that make us suffer. We may wonder: Do I deserve this? If I do deserve it, what does that say about me? Does it mean I'm special? Unique? So much self-consciousness comes into our mind, causing us confusion.

If we know how to organize our thoughts and bring them into our lojong practice, we can minimize our confusion. When we have good fortune, we can be happy with it, but not get stuck in self-absorption as a result. A simple way to do this is to generate such thoughts as "May others have this kind of good fortune, and even more so. May it bring them true, lasting happiness." That resolves the main problem right there.

The emphasis of this slogan is to train our minds to apply these practices as quickly as possible. Doing so will nip our confusion in the bud and greatly reduce our own inner conflict, in the case of both negative and positive things. Whatever we face in our lives, our usual reaction comes out of clinging to a small self. We may think we're not very egotistical because our self-importance doesn't appear in a blatant way. It can be very subtle, yet it is the cause of all our more obvious problems in life.

Our reactions to experiences are like telegraphs communicating something back to our minds. Although our lives are full of variety, the message is always the same: increase care for others and decrease self-importance. From beginningless time, this message has been coming to us, over and over again, but we have always missed it. We have spent all that time innocently but ignorantly absorbed in self-concern. But now that we are clued in to the root causes of happiness and suffering, all we need to do is pay attention and the message will come through.

Whenever we react to external events with confusion, tension, struggle, and pain, that disturbance is a reminder that we need to overcome our self-clinging. When we feel a lack of joy, satisfaction, or meaning in our lives, that is a reminder to increase our care for others. When we notice that we are reacting, it is a helpful exercise to see where that reaction comes from. If we look carefully, we will most likely see the source in one of two tendencies: to self-cherish and to self-protect.

Once we know how to hear and interpret the constant message, it is easy to follow its urging. There is never a shortage of opportunity to step out of the small self and embrace the universal self of all sentient beings. On our meditation cushion, we always have the chance to practice exchange. And in our lives, there are endless opportunities to benefit others. If we are creative and don't dismiss any chance as too small or insignificant, we can live like bodhisattvas.

Some people think that the modern world is not a hospitable place for spiritual practitioners. They dream about being like the great meditators of the past, such as the twelfth-century meditator Milarepa, who lived in a cave and subsisted on nettles. Having a job and a family, being part of the social world—these are just pointless nuisances. But for the vast majority of us, such an escape is just a fantasy. If we are to make any progress on the path of the bodhisattva, we have to do it in the situation we have now, in the environment that surrounds us, among the people in our lives, in the time we are on this earth. This is the perfect time and place for all of us. This is our life. It is what we have on our karmic plate, which is everything we need to progress on the bodhisattva path.

Some say the world is getting worse and worse, but on the other hand, there are so many people caring more and more. The good deeds of many people in each country are what keep the world as safe and comfortable as it is. It's important to recognize this and to rejoice in modern examples of altruism, such as human rights groups, Greenpeace, Doctors without Borders, and animal activists. Whether or not they know they are living the bodhisattva's way of life, these people are carrying out bodhisattva activity through their deeds of caring for others more so than themselves. We need to recognize this and be grateful for all the positive things that are happening in the world.

As long as we take some time every day to settle our mind and reflect on the pitfalls of self-importance and the benefits of altruism, we don't need much more of a lojong practice than what's already going on in our lives. How many times a day do we interact with people, at the workplace, in our family, in our social life? If we have the motivation to step out of our small self, each interaction can be a practice of altruism. We can simply smile, listen, help others feel relaxed, soothed. There is not just one method. We can creatively turn all things into bodhisattva activity. We don't need to be anything more than a mother, a father, a spouse, a friend, a colleague, a fellow human being. Or if we need a break from people, we can direct our love and care toward nature, the animal kingdom, even the insect world. The bodhisattva practice can start anywhere. We can see the lives of any sentient beings as blessings in our own life, allowing us to direct our love and care for the benefit of those beings.

My teacher Dilgo Khyentse Rinpoche never missed a chance to benefit others. He didn't have to set up a schedule. He didn't have to plan the perfect times and conditions to extend himself to others. He didn't wait until the entire row of traffic lights had turned green. Thanks to his creativity and his limitless bodhicitta, every breath in and out was for the benefit of others. We can aspire to live our lives in the same way. Even though we haven't traveled as far along the path, every situation we encounter can lead us in the direction of greater and greater altruism.

If we want to become bodhisattvas, all we really need is some faith in ourselves and inspired motivation. It's a challenging path, but we have all the methods and opportunities we need. If you aspire to be a bodhisattva, if you would love to be a bodhisattva, if you dream of being a bodhisattva, then you already are a bodhisattva.

Point Four

An Explanation of the Practices as a Way of Life

What to Do during This Life

17. The pith instructions briefly summarized: apply the five strengths.

In order to take full advantage of our precious opportunity to progress along the bodhisattva's path, we need to have instructions that give us clarity and confidence in what we're doing. We need a structure for our lives. There are many excellent texts on how to live a life based on bodhicitta, including Shantideva's unsurpassable *Way of the Bodhisattva*. The instructions presented in the *Seven Points* give a more concise structure to support us from day to day, from year to year, and at the end of our life. Both of these slogans (17 and 18) describe five "strengths," which are reliable methods for living and dying like a bodhisattva.

The first strength is *motivation*. In the beginning, a strong, clear motivation drives us to get involved with some kind of activity. Then it keeps us on track, helping us triumph over laziness and inner and outer obstacles. Ultimately it brings us to fruition, to accomplishing whatever we hope to accomplish. Motivation is like having a strong, accurate arm when you want to throw a baseball. Your arm is what sends the ball far across the field, exactly to where you want it to go.

If at a young age you have a vision and a strong urge to become an Olympic gymnast, your motivation can eventually take you there. It's almost laughable to see how young and tiny aspiring gymnasts can be. Some still need help eating and getting dressed. But if they have the right disposition and circumstances, even five-year-olds can develop a strong enough motivation to overcome all sorts of challenges: physical, emotional, and mental. By keeping their motivation close to their heart, by keeping their passion burning inside them, they can develop all the necessary skill and understanding to become an Olympic gymnast. But it's not as though children become Olympic gymnasts just as that thought first enters their mind. To fulfill their vision, their motivation must persist over many years. The same is true for anything. If you want to become a doctor or lawyer, you need to maintain your motivation over many years. If you want to be president of the United States, your motivation must be strong and clear enough to get you past all sorts of obstacles. Barack Obama has said that he wanted to be president from the time he was in elementary school. That shows the power of persistent motivation.

To overcome self-importance and fully develop our bodhicitta also requires a very strong and clear motivation. Just as the young gymnast has a vision of reaching the Olympics, we can have a vision of the peace we will experience when we come out of our absorption in the small self. We will never enjoy this peace as long as our naturally altruistic heart is hemmed in by self-cherishing and self-protecting. How relieved we will feel when we are free from our painful self-centered emotions! We can also foresee the great joy of loving and caring for others, as we grow to regard all sentient beings as our bigger self. And we can imagine how much more effectively we will benefit the world, once we have developed the nondual wisdom of absolute bodhicitta.

If we feel passionate about this vision for ourselves and others, if we clearly see that nothing is more important than developing our bodhicitta to higher and higher levels and eventually attaining complete enlightenment, then before we know it we will get there. And I don't think it will be as hard as becoming an Olympic gymnast, or even a doctor or lawyer. That is because the Buddha's wisdom and methods don't require working with external circumstances beyond our control. Just having our very own mind and following the instructions on internal practices such as tonglen, we can transform ourselves into bodhisattvas. The methods of lojong are intended to work gradually and peacefully. They are a gentle means of making inevitable progress along the bodhisattva path. Once we get the hang of exchanging self and other, once we get a feel for its ease and simplicity, we can make progress in a state of delight, ever motivated to learn whatever we need to learn.

What makes the path especially joyful is that as we step out of our small self, we begin to fall in love with sentient beings. When we fall in love, we can't stop thinking about the person we're in love with. We think constantly about how to make our lover happy. If we see our lover in pain, we can't stop thinking about how to clear away that suffering. We forget about ourselves, which makes us feel so incredibly high, like we've eaten an aphrodisiac. This decreased self-centeredness also gives us tremendous courage. We feel that we can do for our lover things that we never imagined we were brave enough to do for ourselves.

Bodhisattvas are like us ordinary people when we fall in love, but unlike us, their love goes out impartially to all sentient beings. Their love also differs in that it doesn't depend on how their lovers meet their expectations. Their love never waxes and wanes. They are always thinking of others, to the extent that they don't even see a point in thinking of themselves. My teacher Khyentse Rinpoche was incredibly happy whenever he could do anything for others, whether it was small, medium, or large. But when people praised or served him, he was far less delighted. Great bodhisattvas like Khyentse Rinpoche exude joy. You can see it in their presence, in their face, in their eyes. This is the result of their having fallen deeply in love with sentient beings.

The second of the five strengths is *familiarization*. If you've decided to become a gymnast, you have to go through training that involves a lot of repetition. It doesn't matter what your background is or how special you are. You can't say, "I'm a prince, so I shouldn't have to go through rigorous training." You have do what it takes, including accepting feedback. You can't say, "To hell with you, coach. My father is the richest man in the world." If you want to be able to do ten consecutive flips in the air, you have to keep repeating the exercises, more times than Buddhist practitioners say their mantras. Even if all your friends are having fun together, hanging out at the mall or smoking pot, you have to be practicing on those bars and rings. To be able to stick the landing without leaning forward or backward, you have to practice for many, many years. You need familiarization to gain ability, to develop confidence, to learn how to perform under pressure.

To become an Olympic gymnast, you also need to have some innate athletic ability and the right body type. To become a doctor, you need to be strong academically. To become a lawyer, you need a certain level of wits. But to become a proficient lojong practitioner, all you need is determination. Recognizing the cause of your suffering, you are determined to reduce your self-centeredness; and recognizing the cause of joy, you are determined to cultivate an altruistic state of mind. The wisdom and skillful means of these practices are universally applicable, no matter who you are. They are right there to help you fulfill your motivation. All you need to do is practice over and over, gradually acquiring familiarity.

When we practice tonglen, we eventually have to make it our own. It's not enough just to follow instructions from a book but then have our mind go blank as soon as the book is shut. Using self-reflection and contemplation, we need to integrate tonglen into our experience and thereby develop confidence. In the beginning, we develop confidence through working with our mind during formal practice. But eventually, our confidence has to extend to how we are in the world. This is not just a general confidence; it must relate to specific contexts, especially in how we handle the arising of disturbing emotions. When our anger comes up, as it inevitably will, how do we handle it with our practice of exchanging self and other? When we feel insecure, or jealous, or confused, how confident are we in our lojong antidotes? If we apply the strength of familiarization to each of our neuroses, repeatedly, we will develop a stable, unshakable confidence.

Third is the strength of *virtuous seeds,* or merit. In order to fulfill our bodhisattva aspiration to attain enlightenment for the benefit of all sentient beings, we will need a lot of merit to propel us along the path. The basis of this merit always has to be our motivation to benefit others. The clearer our intention, the more merit there is. The intention is more important than the size of the deed or even the seeming benefit to others. For example, if we have a shrine and make an offering of water bowls to the buddhas and bodhisattvas, we can accumulate great merit right there. The enlightened beings have no need of our water bowls, but our pure motivation to step out of our small self makes the act significant. Then, if we have the intention that the merit of this offering bring benefit to beings, that merit increases exponentially. Similarly, any practice we do, such as calming our mind or exchanging self and other, can generate a lot of merit if done with a mind that aims toward enlightenment for the benefit of all sentient beings.

Right now, as we are evolving toward enlightenment, these actions may not seem like much, but we should remember the significance of what we're evolving toward. When we practice with bodhicitta in our minds, we are aiming to become an asset to all the sentient beings in the universe, just like all the buddhas of the past. This kind of asset is much greater than the sun and the moon, even greater than the elements. The sun and the moon and the elements are important to our lives, but what exactly are they doing to liberate beings from suffering? When we become enlightened, we can lead others along that same path, just as the Buddha of our world has done for us. So when you practice, it's important not to think you're just hiding in your room, isolated on your cushion. Enlightenment is greater than anything in this world, and you are determined to achieve that state for the benefit of beings. This attitude can bring so much merit to your practice.

You can accumulate merit in all areas of your life. When you go to work, you can think: "May I practice bodhicitta with everyone I work with and talk to and see. May I serve my employers sincerely and honestly in exchange for the wage I earn. May I use this wage to support others, especially those who would be helpless on their own. May it help bring comfort to others, such as my spouse or my parents." If you have any money left over, you can accumulate merit by donating to charities. A small donation to the Red Cross or an animal shelter can earn you all the merit of what those organizations do as a whole. You can also donate to spiritual centers. Nowadays the education offered by the great universities focuses on skills rather than philosophy. They are producing more effective businesspeople rather than people with wisdom and compassion. Our "higher education" isn't doing much to bring the world out of the darkness of ignorance. Therefore, to contribute to dharma centers, which can't subsist without the support of donors, is incredibly meritorious. Instead of using our earnings exclusively to cherish our small self, we can contribute to vast and profound purposes, thus gaining the joy of both earning and contributing. This can give supreme meaning to having and accumulating wealth.

If you eat nourishing food and do exercise, you can have the intention not just to have an ordinary long, healthy life, but to have more years to practice bodhicitta. Traditionally it is common for practitioners to do longevity rituals, such as prayers to deities like White Tara and Amitayus. In addition, since now we know that good diet and exercise improve health, we can take care of our bodies with the same intention and big vision to lengthen our lives in order to develop our bodhicitta practice. In this way, eating and exercising can be full of merit.

If you have children, you can think, "May I take care of these fine human beings so that they become wise and compassionate and able to benefit others. May I help them in any way I can to remove their ignorance, so that they become assets to the world." If you are kind and compassionate in your social interactions, you can increase your merit by setting the intention to use every situation to develop bodhicitta.

Almost any daily activity offers you a chance to plant virtuous seeds.

Even watching TV can be meritorious if done with the right approach. You can think, "May I watch this program to increase my understanding that I, and my whole world, and all my stories, are just as illusory as a TV show. May this show remind me that all the events of my life have no essence, like the images projected on the screen." In this way, while watching TV, you can also watch your mind. You can observe how you get sucked into the "reality" of the program, even though you know that it's just a play of light. Without losing the fun of watching, you can maintain some awareness of the show's illusory quality.

If you watch a nature show, you can witness how much suffering animals go through. As the salmon is about to go into the bear's mouth, after working its way upstream all the way from the ocean, you can feel touched in your heart. You can then extend that compassion to all the animals on this planet who are eaten by other animals and people. You can observe the relationship between predator and prey and contemplate the workings of karma. Watching TV, reading the newspaper, and other ways of taking in the stories of samsara can become a great source of merit.

Before you go to sleep each night, dedicate all the merit you have accumulated throughout the day for the benefit of beings. Then you can set the intention to practice bodhicitta in your dreams. If you do a little tonglen before falling asleep, it will influence your activities in your dreams, and even they can become seeds of virtue.

Fourth is the strength of *remorse*. Sometimes you have a hard time practicing bodhicitta and accumulating merit. You're not able to be kind to others with your body, speech, and mind. At that point, it's easy to get caught up in judging yourself. That is not productive. As we have discussed, guilt is not a useful emotion. It doesn't help you change for the better. So what should you do instead? To whatever extent you're able, you should openly analyze what is happening. Analyze it objectively, as if it's not even about you. Connect the dots: see what leads to what, how one experience leads to another. Analyze the subtleties of your own and others' ego dynamics, how they play out in your mind and emotions, and how the cure is bodhicitta. Learn from your mistakes, your confusion, your impulses. Learn from your own ignorance. By doing this, you'll be able to see how everything negative happens because of clinging to the self. Then you'll naturally conclude that this clinging is something you should always be vigilant about.

We need to keep observing and reflecting on the destructiveness of self-importance, rather than think we've "got it" after seeing it once or twice. This is a hard lesson to learn. It takes time. We can learn very quickly from physical pain. You can tell a toddler not to touch a hot stove, but the toddler probably will get curious and try it. But as soon as the child feels the sharp pain of the heat, the lesson is learned. With physical pain, it's easier to connect the dots of cause and effect. Emotional pain is different. Unless we meet with teachings that impart genuine wisdom, it's very difficult to figure out where disturbing emotions come from and how to address them.

Many people with a high IQ would fare badly on a test of "EQ," emotional intelligence. Even longtime dharma practitioners can fall short in EQ. Everyone else can see that they're making fools of themselves by clinging to and trying to promote their small self, but to them it's not so obvious. They keep missing the link between cause and effect, between self-importance and grosser manifestations of confusion. Fanaticism, fascism, and cults come from surrendering to the small self without analyzing it critically. These and all other faults come from giving the small self absolute authority over our minds. Our self-cherishing tricks us into thinking it's working for our welfare. But deep reflection proves to us that this is not the case.

The strength of remorse is about increasing your emotional intelligence. When you observe your mind objectively and come to understand the source of all your suffering, you can talk to your self-importance the way Shantideva does: "In the past I was unaware of how you did me so much wrong. But now that I can connect cause and effect, I am different. You can't fool me anymore!"

The fifth strength is *aspiration,* which involves making sincere prayers. What we pray for is to reduce our self-importance and increase precious bodhicitta. We can think about the love and compassion of the buddhas and bodhisattvas, marveling at them and trying to fully understand their strengths and freedom. Then we can pray for those qualities to blossom in our own hearts. In order to help us make aspirations, they have written many prayers that we can recite. We should do our best to say each word sincerely, seeing it as a way to connect with the mind of these enlightened beings and have their qualities grow within us. Even if we use language written by someone else, by contemplating the meaning and speaking sincerely, we make it our own.

Making aspirations in blessed places can enhance their power. If we say prayers at sacred sites, such as the places in India where important events in the Buddha's life occurred, we will see our bodhicitta developing by leaps and bounds. Saying prayers in front of our own personal shrine, or outdoors in a location we feel is blessed by nature, makes our aspirations stronger. Finally, whenever we have done anything positive, anything directed toward the benefit of others, we should dedicate the merit for the growth of our bodhicitta in this and future lives. Dedication is what channels all our beneficial actions into a source of positive energy that can make all our aspirations come true.

What to Do at the Moment of Death

18. The Mahayana instructions for the transference of consciousness are the five strengths. Conduct is vital.

This slogan applies to the end of our lives, when we know that death is near, such as when we are terminally ill. Perhaps our doctors have given us a year or a month to live, or perhaps we have only a ten percent chance of survival. The five strengths are the same as above; however, the order is different.

The first strength to apply to our dying process is that of *virtuous seeds,* the accumulation of merit. At the end of our life, we may have money and possessions. Most likely we'll be attached to these, and our attachments will be a hindrance to a peaceful death. Even in the *bardo,* the intermediate state between this life and our next, our minds can become uneasy about our assets. We may worry about what's happening with them. So what should we do with our money and possessions? Rather than just putting everything in our will, it will benefit us more to relate to them precisely and intentionally, to tie up these loose ends while we are still alive. This will turn a source of attachment and ego-clinging into a source of merit.

As is recommended in the previous slogan, we can give our money to causes that we believe in, such as charities and spiritual centers. We can sell our possessions and donate the proceeds to these causes as well. This will accumulate great merit, both for ourselves and for anyone who has left us money in the past, such as our parents or grandparents. The general recommendation in these teachings is to give at least half of your assets to causes outside of your family because they are likely to benefit more beings, thus accumulating more merit.

What about leaving money to our loved ones? Of course we feel very close to our family and would like to leave something for them. But we want to be intelligent about how we do this. If we leave money to our children but think of them as extensions of our attachment to ourselves, then we will not be letting go of our attachments. This will make it difficult to move on from this life in peace. It is said that beings in the bardo often see their children fighting over an inheritance, or becoming so attached to it that they forget about the person who has passed away. This causes the bardo being tremendous heartache and disappointment. Therefore, if we give money to our loved ones, we should do so with a less attached attitude. If you see your children simply as sentient beings who long for happiness and freedom from suffering, then you can give to them cleanly, with no strings attached. You are leaving your money to *them*—as opposed to other people— because of the karmic bond that you have, but you are not seeing them as extensions of yourself.

Another way of sowing virtuous seeds at the end of life is by going on a pilgrimage, if you are in any condition to do so. The physical effort of making a journey to sacred places can create tremendous merit and purify many of our hindrances and obscurations. Also, doing short retreats—a week, a weekend—will help you get your mind clear about how to approach this last phase of your life. What will not be helpful is to become overly desperate with medicine and treatment after treatment, clinging on until the very end. This will only increase the pain and fear of dying. There's nothing wrong with being reasonably hopeful and doing what we can, but it's more important to develop confidence to let go if the time has come. With confidence, we can rely on the inner strength of our practice and prayers for the comfort and resources that will make our transition smooth.

The second strength is *aspiration*. When we leave this world, we will go like a hair being pulled out of butter. All we will have is this naked mind. So at the end of our life, we should aspire for our mind to be in the best possible condition, full of bodhicitta, suffused with love, compassion, and the noble attitude of tonglen. It is said that the moment just before death will make a great difference in how we travel from this life into the next. If we make aspirations to remember and increase bodhicitta during our dying process and continuing through our journey to the next life, where we hope to meet the teachings and practices of bodhicitta, then we will be creating favorable conditions for this transition.

Third is the strength of *remorse*. The dying process will have a big impact on you, but try not to take it so personally. This is the life cycle of all sentient beings. Virtually everyone who was alive one hundred years ago is gone from this world. So try to take this less as your own tragedy, and more as a universal process and a time to devote yourself to the practice of dharma. If you have any grudges, now is the time to let them go. Even if you can't make peace with everyone, at least let all grudges go from your side so that they don't follow you. If you feel depressed, fearful, or anguished, that is of course normal, but try to recognize that everyone in this position experiences the same things.

See how these natural emotions are the result of our attachment to a small self, and try to use this opportunity as a means to step out of ego-clinging. Make the wish that your current suffering will enable you to destroy your self-importance and go completely beyond it. Since much of your suffering at the end of life is related to your attachment to your body, make the wish that this suffering will help you let go of this attachment. Confess all the activities of your self-centered mind and ask the buddhas and bodhisattvas to help you so that you don't carry this small mind into the next life.

The fourth strength is that of *motivation*. Having established bodhicitta during your life, try to increase it even more at the end of your life. Generating a strong motivation will protect you from being so distracted and scattered by your suffering. It will help you get over the shock of being in the predicament of dying. Recognize that the practice of bodhicitta is your only true friend at this point, the only thing you can rely on. With bodhicitta in your mind, there is nothing to be afraid of, since every other aspect of the mind is merely illusion, merely deception and insecurity.

Finally, there is the strength of *familiarization*. At the end of our life, it is too late to learn new practices. We must take advantage of what we've become familiar with already. If we've learned to work with difficult circumstances, with lojong and especially tonglen, now is the time to put these practices to their greatest use. When we are sick in bed and facing the unknown, we will suffer a lot of anxiety and groundlessness. All our attachments to life, to people, to the world, will show their faces. All our unfinished business will come up, all those mental and emotional issues that we haven't related to in our lives. We will experience many strong feelings, such as loss, doubt, self-pity, anger, discouragement, depression, fear, confusion, and disconnection. These feelings are not the sign of a weak practitioner. They are interdependently originated phenomena, which means they arise when the right causes and conditions come together. The question is, how do we relate to these feelings?

What you shouldn't do is reject or suppress them. If you close down to these phenomena, they will get even stronger. Instead, include them on your spiritual path. Don't spend your last months or weeks running away or distracting yourself. Just lie down on your bed, or wherever you feel comfortable, and open yourself up to feel these emotions.

And then open up even more by thinking about how many beings are suffering in this way. How many have gone through this in the past and how many will go through this in the future? Before you were dying, this kind of suffering was a distant idea. Now you are aware of what others go through. You can see what your loved ones and every other sentient being will experience during the passage of death.

Think about how many people, just in your area, say within one hundred miles, are dying in hospitals. How many people are dying right now in this country, on this continent, in the world? How many are dying in far worse circumstances, such as in wars or epidemics? And how few of the beings who are dying have the support you have, the external support of those who care for you, and the internal support of the dharma? Think about the countless animals dying in slaughterhouses just today. Imagine how great their suffering must be.

Then summon the courage and joy to start the practice of tonglen by mentally taking on all this suffering and adding it to your own. If you are in a state of fear, take on the similar fear of others. Try to locate the "fearer" in your body. You may find a tightness in your chest, which comes from your self-importance, from protecting your ego. This fearer is none other than your small self. It is the one who is anxious, paranoid, angry, confused. Instead of suppressing these emotions, take on the painful emotions of others who are dying. Load them directly onto the fearer, the sufferer.

When you do so, you will find that the sufferer begins to shrink. Your self-importance melts. Before you did this practice, your small self was tightly holding on, desperately thinking about how to rebuild this life, dreaming up hopes of the impossible. Now that you have opened your heart to others through your practice of compassion and tonglen, you can enjoy the tremendous relief and joy of letting go.

To practice giving, the other half of tonglen, touch in with the love and compassion that your pain and fear have brought you. Since your suffering has enabled you to sympathize with what others are going through, it is natural to want to bring them happiness. To the countless others who are dying, give them any peace and joy you have gained through your practice of bodhicitta. Envision them becoming free from suffering, and finding tremendous ease in this transition. To help bring about this vision, make prayers for all beings who must go through death—in other words, every sentient being, without exception—to come to a state of complete peace and joy. Supplicate the buddhas and bodhisattvas to ensure this will come true by the strength of their compassion and power. Then, to fulfill your vision and prayers, offer all your merit for this supreme cause. Offer not only your own merit, but all the merit that has ever been accumulated on behalf of others. You can think of yourself as the enlightened ones' bursar, helping them distribute their infinite merit to those who need it.

The only way to get free from suffering is to remove its condition, self-importance. If, during our dying process, we reduce our self-importance by means of tonglen, our pain and fear will be reduced greatly. It will only flare up again when we start grasping tightly to a small self. At that point, we have to apply tonglen once again.

By practicing tonglen in such a potent time as our approaching death, we can make tremendous progress in a short period. We can make headway against our self-clinging habit, thus removing the conditions for much of our suffering in the future. We have no choice but to depart from this life. But if we go in this way, removing the ground of our suffering and transforming our ordinary mind into bodhicitta, we will make the best use of this time. But it is crucial to become familiar with these methods now, so that we're not jumping into this practice for the first time while on our deathbed.

Toward the very end of our life, we will probably become too tired to do any conceptual practice. We won't be able to think or visualize very well. At that point, we need to rely more on our absolute nature, connecting to it to whatever extent we can. If we have any experience of recognizing and resting in the absolute nature, as described in the second point of mind training, now is the time to put that into practice.

When His Holiness the Sixteenth Karmapa was about to pass away in 1981, he said, "Nothing happens." He was referring to the unborn absolute nature, which is always present, unchangingly. A master such as the Karmapa has no fear of death because he recognizes that both death and life are mere illusions. They have no objective reality; they are just projections of our subjective mind, which gets caught up in what it projects. The absolute nature is the ground for all these illusions, but it itself never changes.

For those who do these practices, the death process doesn't have to be painful or fearful. It can be peaceful and joyful, the opening of a new door and the beginning of a new chapter of bodhicitta practice. I've seen this with my own eyes. For example, when I saw the teacher Lama Urgyen soon after his death, he had a genuine smile on his face, a sign of his joyful bodhicitta. Many others die this way as well. There is no trick to it, other than following the suggestions in this slogan.

In his commentary, Jamgon Kongtrul says, "There are many great instructions for the time of death, but none more wonderful than this." What could be more effective and relevant at a time when you are forced to work with the nitty-gritty of your mind? If you use another method, even from the "highest" Buddhist teachings, but fail to address your self-importance, your clinging will produce continuous suffering. If you don't confront your attachment to the small self, no other method will lead you to peace.

Even if death seems far off, we can familiarize ourselves with the practice of dying by going through this process right now. His Holiness the Dalai Lama said that he does an exercise seven times every day, as if he's really in the situation of dying. If we practice now, then when we approach death, it will seem familiar and natural to us. We will be ready to die peacefully and joyfully.

This slogan gives instructions on how we should conduct ourselves to prepare for the "transference of consciousness" from our mind's current home to the home it will inhabit in our next life. However, if we don't believe in the continuity of life, it is hard to see that our final actions will make any difference. Many people, especially those who are younger and healthy, think it's easier to be an atheist. We're here on Earth for this finite time and then when we die, that's the end. There is nothing more. I find this way of thinking very depressing. It also makes it much more painful to grow older. If you approach the end of your life thinking there will be nothing more, you will feel much more desperate to cling to this life. Your attachment and fear will be much greater. But if you believe in the continuity of life, you can make aspirations to be reborn in favorable circumstances for making further progress along the bodhisattva's path. Even though we have had the incredible fortune to meet the dharma, perhaps we have not had all the conditions to fulfill all our wishes for this life. Perhaps we have often found ourselves in a rut, unable to move forward in letting go of our self-importance. If we make aspirations for our next life, we are likely to find that more doors will be open to us. We will be able to pick up where we left off and go further along the path to enlightenment. This life may be the end of one chapter, but the next life is the beginning of another, even better, chapter.

Once we've begun traveling on the road of increasing virtue, we can feel confident about our next life. There is no reason for us to fear. How do we know if we're on the road of increasing virtue? When we embark on the practice of exchanging self and other, and begin letting go of our habitual self-clinging and replacing it with altruism, our mind becomes more virtuous with each passing day. We create more and more positive karma and less and less negative karma. We may feel like it's too late, that we've already done too many negative things earlier in this life, that we have too many negative habits. But this is not true. Even if we have been self-centered our whole lives and have ignored the inevitability of death, with these instructions we can turn things around very quickly. I would think that our final six weeks could make up for a whole life. Remember the story of the Buddha's past life when he was pulling the cart in the hell realm. With a single altruistic thought he was able to turn his entire karmic situation around, 180 degrees.

Your connection to the dharma in this life is evidence of your karmic evolution. Out of seven billion people on this planet, you are one of the very few who has met these lojong instructions. Even fewer are taking these teachings to heart and sincerely attempting to practice them. Why are you in this rare and precious situation and not others? Unless you believe that things just happen at random, it has to be because of your connection from past lives and the merit you have created because of that connection.

Of course, believing in past and future lives requires faith. This faith, however, is not something foreign to us. It has always been part of the human mind. Even before the religions we know came into this world, people engaged in rituals that related to the continuation of the deceased's consciousness. They prepared the soul to continue on to its next stage. The funerals of the modern world also reflect this deep psychological belief in a future for the deceased. If we didn't have this belief, why would we go to the trouble of having a funeral? Why would we treat a corpse in a particular way if we really had no belief in a continuing mind? Why wouldn't we just dump it in the garbage? Because we feel that treating the body in this way would somehow prevent the soul from being in peace. Do you think that even the strictest atheist would dump his loved one's body in the garbage? Different cultures and people may have their own explanations about death and the afterlife, but this deep emotional belief in continuing consciousness is something all human beings share.

But even though we have this level of faith, having an even stronger and more stable conviction in rebirth will benefit us greatly in the end.

A future life is not something we can see with our eyes. All we can see is that the body has been destroyed. Whether it is buried or burned, the body is no longer a body. But neither does it vanish completely into nonexistence. Every atom continues into the future, combining with other atoms to create new forms and shapes. It is said that the atoms of the Buddha's body are still among us, 2,500 years later. Some of these atoms may be part of our own body. So if atoms, which are made of matter, don't just evaporate, why would we think that our intangible consciousness just vanishes into nonexistence?

Many people think that there is no such thing as consciousness separate from the brain. But what is meant by "consciousness"? Consciousness implies self-awareness. A brain cell is not aware of itself, but your mind is aware of itself. A scientist can put a strange cap on your head and see what areas of your brain are active, but a scientist can't use these methods to find out what you're thinking. But you know what you're thinking. So if you believe that your mind is just made of matter, you are going against your own experience of self-awareness. The brain and the mind do interact with and affect each other, but they are not one. Therefore, the end of the body does not mean the end of the mind.

It may take a lot of effort to contemplate this and other reasonings about rebirth until you feel convinced, but it is a worthwhile endeavor. And whether or not you make this effort, it is a profound thing just to lean your openness to believing in rebirth. Especially if you are older and coming to your final years, I hope you will lean your openness to making aspirations you feel comfortable with. Otherwise, your life may add up to some version of this: "I fed myself, clothed myself, I brought up my kids and sent them to a good college, I laughed a lot, drank a lot, belonged to this or that political party, visited this or that place, had this or that hobby . . ." Even if we've enjoyed a rich and vivid past, at the end of life it seems no more substantial than a dream. And the future is a blank. All we have to look forward to is the loss of everything we hold dear. But if we lean our openness to following the instructions in this slogan, and we make aspirations for our future lives, we can have much to look forward to: having more and more meaningful accomplishments until we reach the ultimate accomplishment, enlightenment.

Even if you are not completely open, but you have doubt or anxiety as you approach death, you can still benefit from the practice of tonglen. Without rejecting these thoughts and emotions, you can take on the suffering of all those who are in a similar position and state of mind. You can breathe in others' insecurity and pain of skepticism and use it to melt the tight grasping in your heart. Feel the relief from your own self-importance and give your peace to others. Offer to others whatever openness and confidence you do have, along with that of all the buddhas and bodhisattvas. Make this offering part of your vision for yourself and all beings to attain complete enlightenment.

One of my teachers, Khenpo Rinchen, used to say that our death will come today. When it happens, it will not be "yesterday" or "tomorrow." It will be *today*. The more we contemplate this crucial topic and prepare our minds, the better off we will be when that "today" comes. We never know when that will be.

Point Five

Measures of Proficiency in Mind Training

19. All dharma agrees at a single point.

When we take a photograph, we first see an image through the camera's lens. We don't press the button to take the shot until we see the image that we want to appear in the photo. Similarly, before embarking on dharma practice, we should start off with an image of what we want our fruition to look like. What is the point of practice? What are we doing this for? It is to liberate ourselves from self-importance, the source of all our suffering and the suffering of every sentient being. If our practice is helping us step out of the small self, then it is in accord with the initial image. It matches the intention of the dharma. If our practice isn't having this effect, then it isn't worth much.

There is nothing wrong with wanting to be well and wanting to be safe. But we tend to take these wishes too far, becoming attached to ourselves in an unhealthy way, which doesn't support us but makes us suffer. We all have a sense of when our attachments—to people, to situations, to ideas—have gone too far and are only harming us. We may even see that they need to be worked on. But the sad story is that we don't often get around to that work. Sometimes we don't know how to work with our attachments; sometimes we just don't want to look at them closely. Either way, our attachments, along with all the other disturbing emotions that arise from self-importance, continue to make us suffer.

As beginning lojong practitioners, we may need to give these emotions a little room. We may need to let them remain at a low level, where they aren't hurting ourselves and others too much. But when these emotions cross the line into neurosis, when they start leading to actions that produce negative results, then it is time to get to our lojong practice.

We can work individually with each of the five disturbing emotions—attachment, aggression, stupidity, jealousy, and arrogance. Or we can relate directly with their source: grasping to the small self. The latter approach is more in the style of the lojong teachings. It is also more efficient: it uses the same rationale as treating a disease by removing the cause rather than by addressing the symptoms. Relating directly with the source requires taking time to sit and notice what is always happening whenever we feel attached, or jealous, or confused. What is the common experience behind these various manifestations? Until we've spent time working with our mind through lojong, it's hard to locate the experience of self-centeredness that is always present. Even when it becomes temporarily clear, the emotions and their related thoughts tend to take over our attention, masking the primary self-importance underneath.

It's like trying to locate and remain aware of the source of a pool of water. When we first see a pool of water, it may take some time to see the spring that feeds it from below. If we sit with any disturbing emotion that comes up and are open to looking for its source, we will eventually be able to see the spring of self-importance. That spring is the source of every aspect of samsara: every delusion, every painful emotion, every negative action, and every difficult circumstance. All of these are part of the pool that comes from the same spring.

When we investigate the source of our suffering, we may encounter resistance in our own mind. This often happens because recognizing our attachment to the self shows us how insecure we are. When we discover the source, we realize that everything coming out of it is, in one way or another, a form of insecurity. In the core of our heart, we have a perpetual spring of insecurity. Witnessing how insecurity continually disturbs our mind can make us hard on ourselves. We may think: "What is wrong with me? Why do I have this condition? Why can't I be like so-and-so, who is always secure and confident?" But "so-and-so" has the same condition. Unless they have thoroughly worn out their self-importance through exchanging self and other and become a supreme being, all sentient beings are insecure in this way.

But it is fine to feel insecure. Every enlightened being has had to work with insecurity. In fact, they became great sages precisely because they were able to make use of their disturbing emotions. Whenever their insecurity became obvious, they were happy to see its face. Why? Because they could then trace the insecurity back to its source and remedy their self-importance at the root. The great lojong practitioners didn't overcome their insecurity through a determined effort to boost their confidence. They did it by working with their attachment to the small self.

To be successful lojong practitioners ourselves, we need to appreciate any chance to discover our own insecurity, seeing it as a pathway to getting to know the root of all our afflictions. Without appreciating this process of discovery, we won't be able to let go of our small self. The process of letting go is not about *trying* to be confident. It's not about trying to be different from who we are. Rather, it's about recognizing our self-importance for what it is, and deciding to stop feeding it.

We can attempt many dharma practices and experience some apparent success with them. For instance, we may be able to calm our mind through meditation on the breath, and thus reduce our afflictions to a minimum. But when self-importance continues to be present, when we fail to address it as the spring feeding the pool, then all our practice will fail to free us from suffering. We can cut all the branches, but if the root remains, the branches will grow back. This is why the relative and absolute lojong teachings are so profound. By emphasizing that the root is poisonous, they motivate us to pull the root out.

It's as if we realize we have a bad marriage to our ego and need to get a divorce. Do we want our divorce to be confused, dramatic, and messy? No, we want a clean and reasonable divorce, based on solid reasoning about how our marriage is unhealthy and unworkable. With as little emotionalism as possible, we want to proceed with firm determination to get out of our bad marriage. Armed with that kind of resolve, we work slowly to get the divorce papers done.

Self-importance, however, will make things much harder for you than a difficult spouse. It will do everything it can to convince you that you shouldn't seek a divorce. It will continually try to undermine your resolve and seduce you back into the unhealthy relationship. And most of the time it will be very persuasive. As a result, our attempts to let go of self-importance may not always work. We may find ourselves confused about what we're trying to accomplish. Sometimes the more we notice our ego-clinging, the worse it gets. What do we do then?

The best remedy is a sense of humor. Don't take your self-centeredness so seriously. Undermine the whole process by laughing at yourself. Recognize the irony: "I want happiness so badly, but my self-cherishing just makes me suffer. Even though I know this, I still can't abandon my attachment to this self!" It's very funny, when you think about it. Life is full of irony. Samsara is full of irony. Mind is full of irony. So try to be witty enough to see and appreciate this irony. Laugh at all your contradictions, especially the contradiction between your intentions and your counterproductive ways of fulfilling them. There's no point in being heavy-handed and feeling so serious about your self-importance. When your habits are so strong that your thoughts and feelings are beyond your control, what else can you do but laugh? Humor is very important in the process of dismantling the ego. Without humor, it's hard to be a practitioner.

The path of lojong is a path of trial and error. Nobody is demanding that we achieve certain marks of progress at certain times. We are just trying our best and being open to what happens. The best lojong practitioners have this kind of humble attitude. His Holiness the Dalai Lama, despite having the highest position of any Tibetan, bows down to everyone. When he is in a panel discussion, he always appreciates the others and has the attitude of being in the lowest seat.

With this kind of approach, progress in lojong flows easily. We don't think of practices such as tonglen as being like harsh medicine: "It may be good for me, but I find it repelling." Lojong isn't at all about being hard on ourselves. It's not about rejecting or being negative toward our ego. Shantideva compares conventional methods, which tend to be harsh, to the methods the Buddha taught. The latter are far more effective because they are gentle and full of wisdom. Lojong is about being wise and appreciating our new understanding of ego. Simply having this appreciation makes us no longer care to keep this tiresome rascal around.

20. Of the two witnesses, rely on the main one.

Things may be going well in your lojong practice. You have gained some freedom, you are having fewer disturbing emotions and reactions, your attachment to the small self has decreased. Bodhicitta has grown within: you are feeling more love and compassion, you are able to practice the exchange of self and other more effectively and sincerely. Now others may be noticing how you've changed. They admire you, praise you, seek your guidance, even want to follow you.

This slogan recommends not relying on such external confirmation. People can praise you one day and scorn you the next. And unless they're omniscient, it's hard for others to detect your ulterior motives. You may be very cunning, good at hiding things from others, conning them. People are often fooled by charlatans, and you may be one of those charlatans. The admiration of others may blind you to these tendencies in yourself.

As new practitioners, we usually seek confirmation from the outside. We want to make a good impression, we want respect. But eventually we realize how painful these hopes are and how little others' confirmation actually benefits us. Even if we are praised, we're still stuck with our self-importance and the suffering it causes. So instead of trusting the witness of others, trust the main witness, your own discerning mind.

Your mind has the power to reveal itself. If you sit down and look honestly and bravely at your own character and motivations, you'll be able to see yourself clearly. If you have sound reasons to be a practitioner—reasons based on recognizing self-importance as your one true foe—you won't be able to fool yourself for long. When you develop a good sense of what is and what isn't dharma, you will have a reliable conscience. Operating from that conscience, you won't want to embarrass yourself by thinking or behaving beneath your own standard as a practitioner. You will maintain decency, always thinking of others and making sure never to harm them. You will be considered decent both from society's point of view and from your own point of view. Not going around with any sense of shame or guilt, you will always be able to walk with your head up.

When you practice exchange of self and other, things change for the better. Rejoice about that and dedicate the merit, but also recognize that there is much further to go. If you make one percent of the progress to enlightenment in this life, that is a lot of progress. But at the same time, there is still the other ninety-nine percent to go. So maintain your enthusiasm to keep practicing. Realize that right now, even if your state of mind has improved considerably, you've only scratched the surface of bodhicitta. Having such a humble attitude will safeguard you from being thrown off by others' confirmation.

21. Always maintain a joyful attitude.

When he was very young, my son told me something very helpful. He said, "Dad, all fear comes from not wanting to lose something." What are we afraid of losing? People, things, our peace, our freedom, our comfort, our choices in life. We're constantly busy trying to ward off these losses. But in lojong, we welcome everything, even the things we conventionally avoid. Because we have methods for working with whatever comes up, nothing is unpleasant, nothing needs to be pushed away. We can be free to be cheerful and unconcerned about the future. Our happiness has no weak point, no hole.

If your house is completely sealed, you can feel comfortable and relaxed, even with a strong wind blowing. But if there is a hole, the wind will come through and stir up dust. When your heart becomes disturbed, when your psychological or emotional state is shaken, it is because you have a hole. That hole is an attachment: to your loved ones, to your possessions, to your reputation, to favorable circumstances. If you notice such a hole but have not yet gained proficiency in lojong, you will probably try to fix it through some form of cherishing or protecting your small self. Such methods have been proven not to work well.

If you learn to let go of your attachment to the self without forsaking your love and care for others, while remaining open to the natural law of the impermanence of all things, you still may feel raw and vulnerable at times, just as everyone does. But at least you won't be suffering because of deliberately holding on to self-importance. You can use that rawness and vulnerability to increase your inspired determination to turn toward relative and absolute bodhicitta. Then you will find yourself living in a well-sealed house, where you feel no threat in your heart. Not having holes doesn't mean you no longer care about anything. It means you are no longer limiting your efforts to the needs of a small self, and can thus increase your love and compassion for the universal self of all sentient beings.

Always being cheerful isn't easy, especially during dark times. Everyone can be cheerful when things are going well, but this slogan refers to unconditional cheerfulness. But when things are difficult, what are our alternatives? Do we have a better choice than to work with our mind with a positive attitude? Our problem is we think we have a lot of choices. This can make us confused, like an overwhelmed child. We may think it's a viable option to hope someone else will take our pain away. But that never works. We may whine and sulk, but that only makes things worse. Once we develop a connection to practices such as tonglen, we realize that having a positive attitude is really the only choice. Then, armed with the resolve of having made this choice, we really do start to feel cheerful, even during the hardest times.

Back in the eighties I heard a story about a man in New York who was terminally ill. He was angry and depressed, especially because he couldn't do the things he wanted to do. When people tried to do things for him, he would get even more irritated. This is common in people with serious illnesses. And his state of mind was getting worse and worse. When his family visited, he would become abusive. They didn't know what to do. So one day his friend asked a Tibetan monk to come over and give him tonglen instructions. The man was very angry at his friend for inviting this bald, maroon-robed man into his room. The monk gave him some simple instructions and then left cleanly.

Over the next few months, the dying man changed. He became more peaceful and friendly, and started expressing gratitude to people. Near the end, he actually felt grateful for his illness. His family was relieved, but they didn't understand what had happened. Finally, his friend asked him what had changed. The man said that for weeks he had been angry about the monk. But after a long period of being stuck in his apartment twenty-four hours a day with his miserable mind, he realized that blaming others and feeling angry wasn't getting him anywhere. He decided to try the monk's suggestion of exchanging self and other, and he found it helpful. The more he practiced tonglen, the more helpful it was. It brought him relief from his pain, anxiety, and reactions. He saw that his pain was not so much from his illness as from his own mind, and that he could address that pain by getting rid of his deep attachments to himself. Then he started thinking about the kindness of others and realized how much of that he had received without acknowledging it. As he began to show appreciation to others, it made him happier and happier, until he felt that he owed his transformation to his illness, which had been so painful to him. He realized that without the illness, he never would have changed. And when he finally died, he was at peace.

22. You have reached proficiency if you can practice even while distracted.

This slogan means that whatever comes up in your life, you can practice lojong without missing a beat. No matter how complex or dynamic a situation is, your mind stays with the vast attitude of bodhicitta, rather than shrinking down to focus on the small, singular self. Sometimes it feels like a force is oppressing your mind from the outside, almost pressing it to react in a self-centered way. Our usual course is to exhaust ourselves by reacting negatively, and only turn to the positive when we are overwhelmed by evidence that this doesn't work. Instead, one who is proficient in lojong is naturally inclined to encounter a difficult situation with a calm, practice-oriented mind, seeing the situation as an enhancement of one's bodhicitta practice.

To be considered proficient, we must also be able to maintain our lojong mind during mundane activities. Even when we are dreaming, our lives are oriented toward others. At some level, we are always thinking of how we can be more kind and compassionate, more generous and patient, more beneficial to our fellow sentient beings. Eventually we can reach the point where there is no gap between our "spiritual practice" and our ordinary life. Both are expressions of our bodhicitta.

To reach this level of proficiency, we need to cultivate two mental attributes: mindfulness of mind and vigilant introspection. Mindfulness of mind (*pagyu* in Tibetan) is like having a surveillance camera watching what takes place in the room of your mind. When we practice a lot of self-reflection we come to see how swiftly our attachment to the self can fly out of control, leading to dangerous emotions such as anger, and the actions that often follow. Seeing how easily our self-importance can transform itself into harming ourselves and others makes us appreciate what's at stake in the practice of lojong. We realize that we're always walking on the edge of a cliff. Understanding this, we feel naturally inclined to maintain pagyu. If we're constantly aware of what's happening in our mind, we can work skillfully with our karma and successfully navigate the path away from self-importance and toward altruism.

Along with pagyu, we need *shezhin,* vigilant introspection. Shezhin is a form of conviction that comes about through analyzing the process by which self-importance causes harm. To develop this conviction, we connect the dots of cause and effect; we see how various attitudes and actions bring about favorable or unfavorable results. Having and using pagyu and shezhin protects us from being a victim of our own mind. When Tibetan Buddhists are about to eat, we recite a chant offering our food to the Three Jewels: the Buddha, the dharma, and the sangha. In this chant, we refer to the dharma as "the unsurpassable protector." This protector is not something outside. It is nothing but our own mindfulness of mind and vigilant introspection, which protect us from all the harm we normally cause ourselves. We are always in need of this unsurpassable protector.

Recently, for example, I've developed a taste for a certain brand of Assam tea. When I asked my friend to get me some, she didn't buy very much, so I felt disappointed. Now, preferring a certain kind of tea in the morning is not necessarily a problem. But if the tea starts running out, and I get anxious about not being able to replace it in time, and I'm wondering how I can live without it, and that anxiety turns into blaming my friend, and I find myself yelling, "Damn it! Why didn't you think of this before?" and I'm filled with burning, violent energy, then maybe my attachment has gone too far. Fortunately, this sequence didn't play out to the end: my surveillance camera was on, and I was able to connect the dots that would lead me to negative results.

There can be a tendency to see self-awareness as a nuisance. We may have subtle thoughts along these lines: "Why not just go along with the habitual unfolding of my mind, even though it may turn into a conflict with someone else?" Or we may think, "This mindfulness is too hard. It feels unnatural. Surely there must be an easier, more free and spontaneous way to live." But if you think this way, all I can say is "Welcome to samsara!" Not making use of our mindfulness and awareness—either through ignorance or laziness—is the brewery of samsara. But if we know what's at stake in our thoughts and emotions, and cultivate the vigilant mind of a proficient lojong practitioner, we will enjoy greater and greater peace and happiness.

Point Six

Commitments of Mind Training

We are now in the sixth point, the commitments of mind training. But before getting into the slogans, I would like to make a few general points about commitments. When I talk about this subject in public, I can often sense the audience's tension rising. We tend to think of being uncommitted as freedom, and commitment as being bound by chains. How can the benefits of committing make up for the restrictions they impose? Why bother with making commitments?

We commit to things that are too important for a halfhearted relationship. Whether it's with our family, our friends, our work, our country, or our spiritual path, a halfhearted relationship leaves a lot of room in our mind for confusion. When we have one foot in the door and one foot out, we are more gullible, more likely to succumb to the tendency to go against our own wisdom and higher interests. The temptations that are always loafing around nearby have a greater opportunity to find the right conditions to hook up with.

Commitments are blessed with protective energy against these forces. This is why so many of the world's great sages, whether religious or not, have made and recommended them. They protect us from our mind's momentum, which can overwhelm us with negativity if left unchecked. If you live near a stream that tends to overflow during the summer rains, it makes sense to dig a trench so that the water won't flood your home. Making the lojong commitments is a way of safeguarding us from the floods of mental negativity. You may be a kind, considerate, soft-hearted person, but if the negative energy in your thoughts and emotions reaches a certain momentum, it can flood the space of your mind. Then you may become confused about why you're thinking the way you're thinking, feeling the way you're feeling, acting the way you're acting. This can lead to strong feelings of guilt. You feel like you can't even have a thought. You want to suppress your mind, but that often leads to an explosion.

The idea of committing to anything can feel like a lot of pressure. And even more intense is the idea of taking a vow. So we should keep in mind that the whole point of making commitments and taking vows is to increase our internal peace and joy. It has nothing to do with being dogmatic or puritanical. We are simply working with cause and effect. Individuals may be puritanical, but that is not the principle of commitments. If we start to feel more pure than others because of our vows, if we make commitments out of one-upmanship, then we are going against the very point of the lojong, which is to reduce our self-importance.

To counteract the feeling of pressure, we should always remember that we are works in progress. We should not expect to do everything perfectly. It's not as if keeping every aspect of every commitment will ultimately make or break us. We should take our commitments seriously, but also give ourselves room to make mistakes. Lojong is mainly a practice of working with our intentions. We are trying to make the gradual shift toward caring for others as much as, and eventually more so than, ourselves. The slogans in this section are commitments to go against the grain. We are working with our mind, something intangible, before it takes shape as external action. If we take vows not to perform certain physical actions, such as killing or stealing, then breaking such vows is quite serious. The traditional image is that of breaking a porcelain vase, which is almost impossible to repair. But when our commitments are focused on mind training, then breaking them is akin to dropping a metal vase. It may get banged up, but a metal worker can make it good as new. On the other hand, it's important not to make commitments thinking that we can break them lightly and then retake them when it's more convenient. This habit will sap our confidence and credibility. We will lose the trust of others, and, more devastatingly, our trust in ourselves.

23. Always train in the three basic principles.

The first of these principles is to stay committed to working against our own self-importance, while increasing our love and care for others. We can start with our immediate family and expand outward to our extended family, our community, and the larger world. It doesn't matter who the object is, as long as the love and care are genuine. But if we extend to others, such as our family members, out of self-importance, it will not work as mind training. To follow this first principle, we need to know precisely what we're doing. We need to identify our self-centered attitudes and decrease them, while identifying our bodhicitta and increasing that.

Abiding by this first principle has everything to do with being mindful of karma, the law of cause and effect. Whatever we have learned through our study and contemplation to be negative behavior— negative in that it is based on attachment to the small self, which makes ourselves and others suffer—is whatever we should avoid. This applies not only to the illustrations of karma found in the lojong teachings, but to all forms of action, big or small. For example, we need to be good citizens and respect our society's laws. We shouldn't run red lights. Some people ask me, "Now that I'm a dharma practitioner, do I still have to pay attention to all these human conventions? Do I still need to vote? Or can I ignore all that?" The short answer is that we should do everything that it is right to do, as practitioners and as members of whatever community we find ourselves part of. We should also respect all forms of spiritual practice that are based on reducing self-importance and increasing altruism. Any teachings that are related to this subject are significant. We should be careful of having too narrow a concept of positive spiritual practice. All we can learn and practice, we should strive to learn and practice.

The second principle is not to use our practice or our supposed understanding of dharma as an excuse to act outrageously. You may feel the urge to test your practice, to see how much of the lojong has gotten into your blood. This may lead you to sleep in cemeteries, or visit places ravaged by epidemics, or act like a daredevil. But there's no point in adopting the outward behavior of a daredevil if you haven't overcome your inner hopes, fears, and self-importance. If you think your outrageous, inappropriate behavior proves that you're going beyond your ordinary sense of self but you haven't yet developed a genuine, mature inner practice based on altruistic mind-set and motivation, you will probably harm yourself and others. There's the story of the fox who saw a lion jump from one cliff to another and thought, "If a lion can do it, why can't I?" But since the fox lacked the lion's natural jumping ability, it fell and broke its back.

In all dharma practice, our motivation forms the ground of everything we do. If our motivation is to be in show business, then our whole practice will be like a Hollywood movie. But if we work on our mind in order to gradually overcome self-importance, then over time the result of our progress will naturally show on the outside. Our practice needs to be rooted in humility and commonsense groundedness. From this basis we can learn to work pleasantly with whatever comes our way, rather than create artificial situations in order to show off.

The third basic principle is to be impartial with lojong, especially in the practice of tonglen. We tend to be biased against certain individuals and not have much patience or tolerance toward them. We shouldn't just practice exchange with the people we respect or those we are close to. We should involve everyone we come in contact with: human beings, animals, even the elements. If we find ourselves developing any kind of partiality in our lojong practice, we should immediately try to remedy that, for all forms of bias come from clinging to the small, singular self.

24. Transform your attitude and remain natural.

The first part of this slogan summarizes all the lojong practices. Before receiving these teachings, our affection is always directed toward ourselves. We take this attitude for granted. It's natural, it's how we're supposed to be. Our affection for others is not as important. It's more dispensable. We also take that attitude for granted. But once we've been introduced to the view of bodhicitta and understand that our self-importance is the root of all our problems, once we have understood these teachings and had some experience of them, we have to transform our attitude by stepping out of the small self and directing our love and care toward others.

In the West, the type of love we value is based on our emotions. When we fall in love, our mind tends to attribute certain qualities to the object of our attraction. We see our new or potential lover as an unending source of bliss. And we think this lover is without significant flaws. These concepts, with the help of our hormones, bring up our desire and lead to a state of euphoria when the object reciprocates. While we feel this bliss, our whole world seems blissed out. But we can't count on that feeling to last long. One day you say "I do," and the next day you're on your honeymoon and realize your loved one snores heavily all night or leaves pajamas on the floor. Since our euphoria is built on unstable ground, it naturally gets affected, no matter how much we work with our mind. The closer we get to the object of love, the more we discover things that go against our initial concepts; the more we discover, the more disillusioned we become.

More stable than ordinary emotional love is *visionary love,* the love of the bodhisattvas. This is based on seeing the equality of self and other. We recognize the other person as a fellow sentient being who desires happiness and freedom from suffering just as we do. Based on this understanding, we commit to doing whatever we can—physically, verbally, mentally—to help the person achieve these states. We dedicate ourselves to this service and see it through, even when there are challenges, even when the person turns against us. As our love becomes cleaner, we naturally feel more joy, even though we are not intentionally focusing on our own happiness.

When we have visionary love, we aren't overly dependent on the presence of our emotions, which are temporary—appearing and disappearing based on many causes and conditions. In other words, not feeling continually and profoundly moved isn't a sign that our love is lacking. No matter how we feel, we can keep moving forward in our care for others because that care has the stable foundation of critical intelligence: our contemplation that all sentient beings are identical at their core.

While transforming our attitude in this way, it's important to remain natural in our appearance and behavior. We may practice tonglen every moment of the day, but we don't have to prove that to anyone. We don't have to show our transformation like a chameleon. Many people would rather change their appearance than their mind. They start changing how they dress and wear their hair. This slogan is saying: If your hair is short, keep it short; if your hair is long, keep it long. You don't have to go around with beads and Tibetan clothing. You don't have to hang conspicuous prayer flags in front of your apartment. Don't turn your home into some kind of museum, which you have to pack up in boxes when your grandparents are coming to visit. If you have a shrine in your home, keep it simple.

You should be able to associate equally well with practitioners and non-practitioners alike. You don't have to show that you're on a different track from others. You don't have to outwardly abandon all your history, all your previous perspectives, like a change of season. If you do these things unnaturally, you won't be able to maintain the show. Even in your spiritual community, always work on the exchange of self and other, but without expecting any special attention because of your efforts. Just be very ordinary. This will give you a tremendous sense of being uplifted. Your natural altruism will speak for itself, and the wind of merit will fill your sails of bodhicitta, carrying you across the ocean of samsara.

25. Do not speak about the downfalls of others.

In the Buddhist teachings, we speak of a person's "three doors": body, speech, and mind. The three doors are the means by which we create positive and negative karma. Since body and speech are more tangible than the elusive mind, they are easier to control. If we can't control our body and speech, how can we ever hope to control our mind?

This slogan focuses on our speech, which tends to be more of a problem for us than our body. It's much easier for our mind's activity to manifest through our speech than through our body. As my teacher Dilgo Khyentse Rinpoche put it, "Speech is the way all our filth comes out."

We often speak of others' downfalls: "This person has this fault. This person does this wrong. Therefore, this person is not good. And everyone should be aware of it." Our criticism may extend to the dharma: "This person doesn't practice enough. This person is not a good practitioner. This person doesn't have enough devotion, commitment, and so on. This person is supposed to be a practitioner, so they shouldn't act like this. They should be beyond this." The object of our criticism may or may not have these downfalls. It doesn't matter; the important thing is to keep our own speech from going in the wrong direction.

Sometimes we act as if we've been assigned to announce the faults of others. We may believe we're protecting people from harm by denouncing those we disapprove of. Or in some situations, especially as a parent, teacher, or friend, we may feel like it's our duty to correct someone. But before you say anything "helpful," check your motivation. Make sure you're not merely trying to satisfy yourself. And even if you find that your motivation is pure, make sure the person you want to help is open to that help. If everything is favorable, then you can say what needs to be said. But simply coming down on someone and speaking about their faults will only make everyone upset. That will not do any good.

We should also be wary of our speech when we're innocently chatting with our friends. Just to make conversation, it's natural to start talking about people we know in common, which can easily slip into a discussion of their faults. This can easily lead into damaging gossip. Why do we do this? Often it's because we find such conversation exciting. But if we keep our mindfulness of mind and our vigilant introspection close at hand, we can prevent ourselves from going too far. In these situations, Shantideva recommends "being like a log." When you notice this kind of excitement coming on, just be still and let that whole energy calm down. That will save you from doing a lot of harm with your speech. The point of this slogan is not to be uptight or puritanical. As with all the lojong teachings, it is to prevent our self-importance from gaining the upper hand, bringing suffering to ourselves and others.

26. Do not ponder others' business.

Being sloppy with our speech is not only harmful in its own right. It also perpetuates our harmful habits of mind. Careless speech leads to careless mind. But it goes both ways. Careless mind also leads to careless speech. This slogan is the mirror image of the previous one. It focuses on cleaning up the kind of "filth" in our mind than can easily come out in damaging words and actions.

Our minds naturally get attracted to thinking about what others may have as faults. This can become an addiction, especially for those who have a lot of pride. And when we discover these faults, we're naturally interested in pondering them. Being nosy about others' business can be exciting or even contagious. But this habit causes a lot of suffering in our mind. When we look at others with critical eyes, we create a birthplace for being unkind. Critical thoughts naturally lead to feelings of resentment. And when our criticism is directed toward people close to us, we begin to push them away, to extricate ourselves from them, to isolate ourselves.

This slogan, however, is not suggesting that we reject our critical intelligence altogether. We depend on our critical intelligence to understand others and our relationship to them. But when we use this intelligence simply to be critical, merely out of the habit of scratching an itch, we endanger both our lojong practice and our relationships with others. So when our pondering habit rears its head, we need to apply some discernment in order to work productively with our minds.

It's important to note that we're not trying to be forceful with our mind and suppress our negative thoughts. We are simply noticing that we have an addiction and trying not to indulge in it. When a negative thought about someone arises in your mind, let it come out and show its face. Let yourself feel the pain of it for a moment. Remember where critical thoughts can lead you, where they've led you so many times in the past: to harmful words and actions, to rejection and isolation. Then apply an antidote.

We can first reflect on how all our perceptions are subjective. No two people see things in the same way. Even the Buddha was seen as a person filled with faults by his jealous cousin Devadatta. There are infinite ways of looking at someone. Because of our bias, we may not want to believe this. We may deny that what we see so negatively is not inherently negative, that there is always a positive side we can focus on. But when we contemplate the results of thinking critically of others, we can give ourselves the incentive to at least balance our negative thoughts with positive thoughts.

So try to think about the person from someone else's point of view. This person you are so critical of has relationships with many other people than yourself. Some see this person in a negative light, some in a positive light. Try to have more respect for the positive point of view. Try not to think that your own perception is the truth, the whole truth, and nothing but the truth. And if you focus on someone's good qualities but still can't come up with a single one, you can at least reflect that all sentient beings are identical at the core. All of us have the potential to overcome our self-importance and become a tremendous benefit to other sentient beings. This potential may be deeply hidden, but it exists in every one of us. We all have the potential to attain complete enlightenment. So even if you can't think of anything good about someone, you can at least give them credit for that. Changing your focus to the person's positive qualities is a bit like distracting a child who's throwing a temper tantrum. You say, "Oh, look here, look at this!" and the child forgets what he or she was so upset about.

27. Train with the strongest emotions first.

These troubles, and most others we encounter in our lives, come about when our mind is under the influence of self-centered emotions. When we find ourselves speaking of others' downfalls or pondering their business, we have the opportunity to look at our minds to see which of these emotions is the main cause. Once we discover which emotion is at fault, we can apply a remedy. Since all our disturbing emotions come from self-importance and are therefore interlinked, as we make headway against our most prominent form of negativity, it will help us with all the others.

Negative speech and thinking are often the product of arrogance. To maintain our imagined status above others, we indulge in criticism. Now, arrogance may not seem like a painful emotion because it often comes with a quality of feeling high. But when we're arrogant, we often need external confirmation about whatever it is we're proud of. That need makes us insecure. Out of insecurity, we get all wound up trying to sell ourselves for something insignificant, such as praise for being good-looking, or smart, or unique. What we achieve from such confirmation is tiny compared to what we go through in order to obtain it, and to keep it going with constant self-promotion. So, when we're feeling arrogant, we must apply the remedy of humility. We can achieve this through the "exchange of position" practice described in *Point Two*. Or we can contemplate how ourselves and all other beings are identical in terms of our desiring happiness and freedom from suffering, and in our equal potential to attain enlightenment.

Sometimes our critical mind comes from jealousy. We envy someone or want to compete with them. This emotion makes the person a threat, even if they have never done anything wrong. When we connect our negative speech or thought process to jealousy, we can be happy that we have discovered the culprit. Then we can apply a remedy. Again, we can practice exchange of position, which also counteracts jealousy. Or we can simply rejoice in the other person's good fortune, knowing that they want to be happy just as much as we do.

Aggression is often the cause of our fault-finding behavior. Someone has done something to us that we don't like. However, we don't feel justified in outwardly lashing out, so we ponder, ponder, ponder. If such is the situation, we have to realize that no amount of pondering will help. This could go on unresolved for decades, or even lifetimes. When we hold on to a grudge for so long, it is because we're not fully conscious of the pain it brings us. But once we're aware of the pain, applying an antidote to our aggression becomes the sensible and obvious thing to do. The more we practice lojong, the easier it becomes to notice when we're causing ourselves suffering. It is said that ordinary people notice their pain at a similar level to noticing an eyelash on the palm of their hand. An advanced practitioner, on the other hand, notices pain as if it's an eyelash on their eyeball. The quicker we notice, the quicker we can apply a remedy. It is very straightforward. We are simply doing ourselves a favor.

To remedy aggression, we can apply tolerance. We recognize that the person's actions and our being hurt by them are the result of past karma. This karma is not a simple, linear cause and effect. Many, many interconnected causes have had to come together in order to produce the current situation. Therefore, there is no point in placing heavy blame on any one cause. It is biased, unfair, and fruitless. An infinite web of interdependence is at work, and we are part of that web just as much as the other person is.

We can also remedy aggression by reversing our psychology. Usually, we reject any offense and feel angry. But being offended can be good for us. By working with it, we can become stronger and less reactive;

more tolerant, calm, and clear. Instead of feeling resentment, we can rejoice. Another remedy is to cultivate aggression's opposite emotion, compassion. We contemplate the other person's suffering and sincerely wish that they become free of all pain and its causes. As Shantideva points out, we are one of those causes. Those who harm us have only come into our lives because of harm we have done them in the past. When we consider that their angry lashing out will bring them even more suffering in the future, we can feel compassion and wish them freedom from pain. Directing our mind toward a positive emotion and away from a negative one is like putting a cup of cold water into a pot of boiling water: it dramatically reduces the heat. When we become proficient at applying these remedies, we can feel immediate relief as soon as we begin to apply them.

You will be surprised at how malleable your heart and mind can be if you truly want to be free and take the time to engage your mind in this way. With such techniques available to us, it makes no sense to hold on to resentment for one hour, or even one minute. Every hour and every minute is part of our precious life, so why not live it in peace?

Speaking ill of others and pondering their faults may also come from attachment. We can be so possessive, so territorial, so attached to this small self. We can be so unreasonable in wanting everything to be the best for *me*. In this state of mind, the whole of humanity falls into two categories: those who are on our side, and those who aren't. But being attached makes it impossible to have space in our mind. When we have mental space, we can think about something when we want to and not think about it when we don't want to. But when we are so attached, we lose that basic ability to choose what our mind is doing. This prevents us from ever being carefree, and instead makes us feel weak, overwhelmed, exhausted. We usually think that hard work is what makes us so tired. But we don't feel so exhausted when we're exerting a lot of physical energy doing something we enjoy, such as riding a bike or hiking up a mountain. It's only when our mind is attached that we feel so fatigued.

Sometimes we don't want to look at our attachments in a clear light because we're afraid of having to let go. But what does it mean to "let go"? Letting go has nothing to do with the thing itself. It is about letting go of the attachment. We have to be careful in differentiating the object from the attachment. We don't want to lump the two together. The object is something that we can enjoy, if we have a healthy relationship with it. Attachment, on the other hand, only brings us suffering.

It is like having a string tied to our heart that connects us to the object of our attachment. No matter where we go or what we do, we can't enjoy ourselves because we feel the constant tug of that string. We may be on vacation in Paris, with time and freedom to wander around enjoying ourselves. But if we are worried about the valuables we have left in the hotel room, our pleasure will be spoiled by that painful tug.

We can see this most poignantly in overprotective mothers. All mothers are naturally attached to their children, but when their attachment is excessive, motherhood becomes a torment rather than a joy. Instead of appreciating their children and being enriched by the experience, a lot of mothers and fathers mainly experience the dark side of parenthood.

Attachment may be the most difficult emotion to overcome, but we can make progress by continually observing how it brings us suffering and does us no good. In place of our attachment, we can cultivate a less self-centered love, a visionary love that is tuned in with the actual best interests of others. This kind of love often involves letting go. For instance, if penguins don't let go of their young at some point, the little ones will never grow up to be competent adult penguins. They will never be free to live fully. By letting go, the parents are not rejecting love and care, but expressing a higher form of love. As lojong practitioners, we can cultivate visionary love for those close to us, and then spread that love among all sentient beings, simply because they have the same desire to be happy that we do.

Mushroom hunters are passionate about mushrooms. Archaeologists are fascinated by past civilizations that have been buried under the earth. Mountain climbers love the experience of being in high, thin air. For the lojong practitioner, the most significant joy is in investigating our self-importance and all the ways it manifests, such as these disturbing emotions. The great Buddhist masters are like passionate scientists in the way they examine their minds. They love to study how their emotions come about, and they enjoy taking each of them apart, piece by piece. These practitioners analyze their emotions objectively, without any self-judgment, knowing that every emotion is universal. They could have the most horrible thought of anger and still see it as universal.

As beginning lojong practitioners, we should aspire to having this objective approach toward our own mind. Speaking ill of others or pondering their business are two clues that we are clinging tightly to our small self. These and other egocentric actions should make us aware of the underlying emotion that is causing us pain, whether it be attachment, aggression, or jealousy. And ultimately we would like to cut off the tendency to criticize others at its very root. In order to do so, we need to go deep within and locate our self-importance. At that point, we can then apply the greatest remedy of all: tonglen.

28. Abandon any expectation of fruition.

Think about a summer garden full of beautiful flowers. What made these flowers bloom? It was the seeds, the weather, and the hard work of the gardener. With these conditions in place, flowers will bloom, regardless of anyone's hopes and fears. And without these causes and conditions, the garden will be a failure. Similarly, happiness and freedom from suffering arise when the necessary causes and conditions are there, and don't arise in their absence.

The lojong practices, when done with the proper motivation, generate merit, which naturally brings us favorable results, such as a good reputation and increased comfort. Our hopes and expectations for these types of fruition don't contribute at all to a positive outcome. In fact, because these hopes are focused on the small self, they undermine our practice and actually prevent us from receiving its benefits.

The practice of bodhicitta eventually leads us to complete enlightenment, which is of immense and lasting benefit for the universal self of sentient beings. When we place our hopes in minor accomplishments, such as getting credit for being a good person, or even having a better rebirth in our next life, we are shortchanging ourselves. When we let our ego get hooked into relatively petty expectations, we make it that much harder to get free. The taint of self-importance severely limits the effect of our practice.

This slogan encourages us to simply practice lojong for its main purpose of reducing our self-importance and increasing our altruism. The results will take care of themselves. If they don't come immediately, there's no need to feel despondent. That will only decrease our motivation for practice and allow our negative habits to take over. If we start to slump into depression, we can apply the teachings for taking difficulties onto the path. Eventually, thanks to the natural and inevitable workings of cause and effect, we will overcome all obstacles and enjoy lighthearted freedom from the tyranny of self-importance.

29. Abstain from toxic food.

If you prepare a delicious meal, but one tiny drop of poison gets into it, that meal will be spoiled. No one will be able to eat it. In this analogy, the meal is our practice of bodhicitta and the poison is self-importance.

But here I would like to make an important clarification. When we speak of "poison," we are not speaking of self-centered thoughts just popping into our mind. We don't have control over what thoughts pop into our minds. That is not up to us. For example, we may be practicing tonglen and discover ulterior motives that have infiltrated our mind stream. But if the surveillance camera of our mind is on and we see unfavorable thoughts arising, it is up to us how we relate to them. We can choose not to make a big deal about them, let them go, and continue with our practice of bodhicitta. Or we can take them seriously and, as a result, act out of attachment to the small self. The latter is what is meant by "toxic food."

When our actions are based on thoughts and emotions of self-importance, when the whole point of what we say or do is based on promoting a self-centered agenda, then we are going against this lojong commitment. Instead, if we keep ourselves from acting until we can reset our intention to something positive, we can enjoy delicious meal after delicious meal.

30. Do not be a loyalist.

Loyal friends are always kind, supportive, and understanding. Whatever we ask of them, they will do their best for us. When it comes to relationships with others, loyalty is an excellent quality. But it is the opposite when it comes to how we relate with our ego. With others, we should be helpful and agreeable, but with our small self we need to stop saying "Yes, sir" or "Yes, ma'am."

Right now it's as if we have a tremendous amount of funds, which we are mostly allocating to our self-importance. Our small self is not only wasteful with those funds; it is totally ungrateful. Not only does it fail to appreciate our generosity; it constantly causes us trouble, using all its tricks to dupe us into confusion and ignorance. When we recognize how this rascal treats us, we naturally want to stop supporting it. But what should we do with all our funds? We can reallocate them to our care for others. We can stop sending them to the corrupt department and start sending them to the noble department.

We can train our minds the way some parents train their children. Say a boy has the bad habit of sticking his fingers between the hinge side of the door and the door jamb. The mother keeps telling him not to do it, but he doesn't listen. Finally, the door closes and his fingers get hurt. The boy screams and cries, but the mother says, "I told you not to do it. I'm glad this happened. It's a good lesson for you!" This is what we should do with our self-importance. When cherishing and protecting our small self gets us into trouble, we can appreciate the feedback and think of it as a valuable lesson. We can have this approach with any negative circumstances that come up in our lives. Even if we can't trace back how our self-importance has led to our being harmed, we can be sure that at some point, perhaps in a past life, this ego is to blame.

In *Training the Mind and Cultivating Loving-Kindness,* his commentary on the *Seven Points,* Chögyam Trungpa Rinpoche translates this slogan as "Don't be so predictable." Our ordinary way of reacting to circumstances is very predictable. We invariably side with our small self. A good example is how we hold grudges. When we hold a grudge, we are being too understanding of our ego. We're making a case for it and a case against someone else. We're willing to sacrifice our peace of mind and well-being, willing to enter the war zone and stand in the line of fire, all for the sake of our small self. If you're shot by an arrow and the arrow comes out, how intelligent is it to stick the arrow back in your wound and grind it around, over and over again? Holding onto a grudge is equally intelligent. The unpredictable response would be to realize how it's more important for us to have a clean heart than to justify our grudge. If we forgive the other person, and on top of that wish that person to be happy and free from suffering, we are practicing the great intelligence of disloyalty to our small self.

31. Do not be contentious.

This is a sequel to the previous slogan. When you find yourself being fired upon, don't fire back. Don't attack the other person verbally. If you do, the other person will fire back again, and you will fire again, and so on. If you meet abuse with abuse, things are likely to get out of control. Both people can hurt each other, much more so than they intended to. So avoid getting into heated arguments.

Also, avoid maligning others to a third party. You may find someone who has nothing to do with the problem, a friendly ear who is willing to listen to you vent. But after a while, that person will start to think, "Why do I get the privilege of hearing this over and over again?" It becomes unpleasant to hear you continually vent and emote. When you subject a friend to whatever's going around and around in your head, you're probably not thinking about whether your friend has the time to listen, or whether your friend may even be getting disturbed. Out of self-absorption, you are being inconsiderate. If you keep going in this way, you'll have double trouble: trouble with the original person who made you angry and trouble with your friends who don't want to hear any more venting. So it's best to stop this behavior before people start avoiding you. Instead of venting, recognize that the grudge comes from loyalty to your small self, and work on forgiveness.

32. Do not wait in ambush.

Again, this slogan is related to grudges. Let's say someone hurts you, but you don't have a chance to retaliate. Perhaps you are too weak now, or the circumstances aren't right, or it took you a while to even realize you were harmed. So you wait for the right time to strike back. If you were fighting in a war, you would be looking for the perfect position: say, a narrow gorge where you could set up some machine guns. With such an ambush, a few men can kill hundreds.

The prospect of setting up an ambush may seem exciting. We can spend years maneuvering in our mind, planning out the perfect way to take advantage of our strengths and the weaknesses of our enemy. But such activity is actually masochistic. We may think we are enjoying it, but in fact we are continually disturbed. The grudge is eating us up. And every thought about our plan creates negative karma, bringing us further out of touch with our altruistic heart. Waiting in ambush is a horrible strategy for our bodhisattva path. So when we find ourselves imagining striking back, we must see this as a golden opportunity to thwart our self-importance. We can reverse the momentum of our small self and use this challenging situation to increase our bodhicitta.

33. Do not pounce upon vulnerability.

Martial artists know the human body's pressure points. By striking these vulnerable spots, they can cause crippling pain or even death. This slogan is about the emotional equivalent of pressure points: insecurities. If we know where someone's insecurities lie and we attack those points verbally, we can cause tremendous pain.

Most of the time, of course, we try not to take advantage of others' insecurities in this way. But in some situations, such as during a heated argument, or when we feel unstable or troubled, we may go for those vulnerable areas. And instantly, a lot of trouble arises. So we need to have the mindfulness, discipline, and integrity to avoid such behavior.

We can pounce on vulnerability either harshly or "diplomatically." While exposing someone's deepest weaknesses and insecurities, we can speak violently or adopt a gentle, honey-tongued manner. Sometimes we do this not out of pure malice, but because we are so intrigued by where the conversation will take us. We feel compelled to go down this road, even though we know it will lead to disaster. We choose ignorance over wisdom, pain over peace.

Every conversation has its own boundaries of sanity. When we sense we're going beyond these boundaries, to the point where it will soon get painful, then it's better to change the topic to the bees and the flowers and the weather. This approach seems to go against the consensus of modern psychology. Many people think that avoiding pressure points means avoiding deep, honest communication. But in order to have these conversations, the people involved must be open to the topics. They need to have the strength of mind to bear a conversation that exposes their insecurities. Otherwise the dialogue will just cause unnecessary pain.

Before getting into these conversations, we need to work with our own minds. If both people have worked with their minds and are open to learning from each other, then this kind of honest communication can take place. Both people will be able to hear what the other person has to say. But there has to be mutual openness. Both participants need to trust each other and be interested in self-reflection and seeing their own faults. Without this interest, the conversation will be filled up by self-cherishing and self-protection. There will be no space for honesty and no way to make space—it's not as if you can just drill a hole.

34. Do not transfer the dzo's load onto the ox.

A *dzo* is a cross between a yak and a cow. Dzos are stronger than cattle and give more milk. Because Tibetans are so dependent on milk and butter, the productive dzo is a very precious animal. A person who owns five dzos is considered wealthy. Oxen, on the other hand, are not as highly cherished. On a journey, an ox will have to carry a larger load, even though it is weaker than the dzo. Tibetans tend to worry about the dzo: "I hope my precious dzo doesn't get worn out. I hope my precious dzo doesn't have to go through too much. I'm so concerned about my precious dzo." But the ox's well-being isn't as important. Even if the ox dies, it's easy enough to go buy another one. So there's always a tendency to put more and more of the dzo's load onto the poor ox.

In this analogy, the concern about the dzo is like our excessive care for our precious self. We are so careful and protective of this small self, always trying to foresee dangers and take precautions to avoid them. The callous attitude to the ox is like the way we habitually ignore the welfare of others. What they have to go through is insignificant compared to what happens to us. A small suffering that we may have to experience matters much more than a large suffering for somebody else.

With this attitude, we tend to shift our responsibilities onto other people, even if they are less capable of handling them. Using our skills, our charm, our sneakiness, we figure out a way to make someone else deal with whatever makes us feel burdened or uncomfortable. When we fail at something, instead of owning up to our failure, we blame others. To avoid taking the blame ourselves, we make all kinds of excuses or we purposely create confusion to get off the hook. Since we don't care as much about others, we make them take the consequences of our actions. Even if we only need to say sorry, we try to get out of saying sorry.

This slogan encourages us to take responsibility and admit our mistakes. The Japanese culture is very strong in this way. Even the emperors take pride in apologizing when they are at fault. They bow down low and say, "I'm very sorry. It was my mistake." Having this quality gives people tremendous freedom and dignity. Not subjecting ourselves to the uncomfortable tension of creating excuses enables us to maintain high self-esteem, even when we have done wrong.

Transferring the load onto others starts as early as childhood. I've seen four- and five-year-olds do this. They aren't taught how by their parents, but somehow they figure out how to use their strength, or beauty, or confidence to manipulate others. But using our skills to avoid unpleasant situations makes us weaker and weaker. We become more and more dependent on others. This can go on throughout our lives, even into our eighties and nineties. There are couples in which one person seems incapable of getting up to fetch something or opening up a door by themselves. An "uncivilized" person who saw this behavior would probably think, "Is there something wrong with his feet? Is there a problem with her hands?" Being so codependent makes us very insecure. We know that one day our whole system will collapse. One day we will no longer be able to say, "Honey! Do this, do that!"

As lojong practitioners we have to become conscious of these tendencies and behave in a more altruistic way. Since we have effective practices for bringing difficult situations onto the path, we can stop trying to avoid them. If we remember that it's in our best interest to continually practice the exchange of self and other, we will no longer be tempted to transfer our burdens onto others. We can even go so far as to accept blames and responsibilities that aren't ours.

35. Do not be competitive.

If you run in a marathon or ride in a horse race, you try to get to the finish line before everyone else. That is the appropriate attitude because you are playing a game. But if you take this approach to other areas of your life, there will be lots of trouble. Always trying to get ahead of others makes it hard to live with yourself. When you lose the competition, you are disappointed. When you win, people resent you. Your competitive attitude prevents you from rejoicing in others' success, so you can't be a good friend. It becomes very difficult to connect with others.

Some people feel like they can only thrive when they are being competitive. For them, competition is an addiction without end. If they win at the junior level, they have to compete at the senior level. Then there's the college level, and then the professional level. It goes on and on. And if they somehow come out on top of everyone in the world, they discover that they're tremendously lonely.

We can compete with others in any area: good looks, education, fame, reputation, wealth, standard of living, and so on. If the competition is taken too seriously—which is even the case when it comes to most games—we can't settle our mind and be content. We can never be totally at ease.

Competition is an especially bad habit when it comes to the dharma, since the whole point of our practice is to work with our self-importance. Competing to say the most mantras or do the most prostrations, studying in order to know more than others, trying to beat everyone else in a race to enlightenment—how will any of these pursuits bring peace to our minds? All they will accomplish is stronger clinging to the self, and therefore more suffering.

In the conventional mind-set, being aggressive to go after what you want is a desirable quality. But having such a drive requires a kind of willful blindness. If you pause and consider whether your competitive drive is really going to bring about happiness, you may endanger the rationale for how you spend your life. You may lose your orientation as to where you're going. If you look into the lives of others who are overly competitive, you may discover that they are also in a state of constant turmoil. So you avoid questioning your drive and instead keep fueling it with your attachments, which continually give you reasons to keep going.

This slogan encourages us to question our competitive drives. If we have already studied and contemplated the relative merits of self-importance and altruism, we should be more willing to take an honest look. Then we can remedy our competitiveness by rejoicing in the success of others. We can enjoy all that is available in this world without having to think of it as *mine*.

36. Do not twist the practice.

The lojong instructions encourage us to accept loss as a way of reversing our habitual attachment to the self. This slogan encourages us not to implement such precious teachings in a twisted way. For example, when people—especially couples—argue, it is common for one of them to become silent. The other person shouts and shouts until he or she feels exhausted or embarrassed and then gives up. The quiet one then thinks, "Hmm, this silence has paid off. I've won!"

People who speak less have the advantage of exposing themselves less. Those who have to convert every thought and emotion into speech tend to make more messes. When these two types clash, the silent one is likely to come across as a better, saner person. The expressive one probably will be the one who apologizes. But when it comes to the issue itself, whichever part you play doesn't determine if you are right or wrong. It takes two to tango. Cunning people can use silence as a passive-aggressive way of dominating a relationship.

This is not to encourage you to get into heated arguments. It's rather to discourage you from using your mind deceitfully. Letting people shout at you so that they make fools of themselves is not the same as genuinely accepting loss. It's more like appearing to take a loss in order to secure a victory. When you deceive others in this way, you are not practicing lojong. You are practicing manipulation.

There are other ways to twist the practice that we need to watch out for. For example, we may do a practice such as tonglen for the sake of a better "me." Instead of using tonglen to let go of self-importance, we use it for our own ego's healing or protection. Our aim is to improve the small self instead of overturn it as the destructive rascal that it is. Practicing tonglen in this way is not effective because it misses the whole point, to exchange self and other.

When we twist the practices, our action does not meet our intention. Instead of moving toward freedom, we move toward intensified bondage. It's like knowing that your guest will be arriving at the eastern gate, and then going to the western gate to receive him. We should do our best to avoid this kind of confusion.

37. Do not bring a god down to the level of a demon.

Let's say that you actively worship a god by praying, making offerings, and attending rituals. If that god is powerful and benevolent, you will receive care and protection. But if, instead of venerating, you mistreat the god, you may find that god turning against you like a demon. The purpose of dharma is to become free from the bondage of our self-importance and to enjoy the peace of embracing the universal self of all sentient beings. This path can lead us to higher and higher rebirths until we become bodhisattvas and eventually buddhas. If, however, we use dharma to gratify our ego, then we are mistreating these sacred teachings. It is like asking a god to do your dirty work. Engaging in any form of spiritual materialism is like bringing a god down to the level of a demon.

These days, every one of us needs to be careful about this tendency. If we find ourselves thinking, "I have accomplished this and that, and I know lojong better than others, and I can help shed light on others' shortcomings," then we should realize that we are practicing anti-lojong. Such arrogance defeats the whole purpose of these teachings. This is not to say we should be exempt from having any of these thoughts. That is unrealistic. But we need to keep an eye on these tendencies and not let them run loose in our mind.

We should also be careful not to take such pride in the lojong that we look down on other religions or other Buddhist practices. If we become religious fanatics, then again the whole purpose of mind training is missed. Self-importance comes out on top. Instead, we should think of ourselves as the lowest of all beings. This is not an attitude of low self-esteem. In fact, it is the opposite. If we put ourselves in the lowest, humblest seat, we remove any chance of feeling insecure. From the lowest seat, there is no place to fall down. Such humility naturally comes with a sense of nobility, which enables us to focus on other beings and bring them great benefit.

38. Do not seek out others' suffering as the limbs of your delight.

There's a famous story about two scholars in a Tibetan monastery. These scholars, both monks, had a rivalry. One day, one of them said to his attendant, "Make some nice tea. I have good news." The servant made a delicious cup of tea, served it to the scholar, and asked about the news. The scholar said, "My rival has a woman in his life!" He was overjoyed that his rival would now be disrespected. When a great teacher living at that time heard this story, his face went dark. He asked, "Which of the two scholars' behavior was worse—the monk who broke his vow of celibacy, or the one who rejoiced in his rival's downfall?"

If we are on the bodhisattva's path, aiming to shed our self-cherishing and cultivate altruism, then we should never hope to benefit from others' misfortune. If we know that someone is suffering, but we are fixated on how we might gain from the situation, then we are training our mind to become even more self-important. There are many ways of doing this. Doctors can hope for patients to get sick so that they have more income. Businessmen can wish for their competitors' business to suffer so that theirs will do better. Sons and daughters can hope for their parents to die so that they can inherit money. Some people even profit from war. When we are obsessed with our small self, we become blind to others' pain and fail to pay appropriate respect to what they go through.

After the successful resolution of the Cuban missile crisis, President Kennedy discouraged people from gloating. He acknowledged that many people had gone through a lot of suffering and that it therefore would be disrespectful to gloat. His attitude was in line with this slogan. Similarly, in 2003, when the former king of Bhutan was able to expel most of the foreign terrorists from his country—a feat that India didn't think possible—his army and the rest of the kingdom wanted to celebrate. But he asked his people not to throw one party or hoist one flag in celebration. He felt it was more decent to remember all the people, from both sides, who had died in the conflict.

In a more subtle way, even teachers of the dharma may seek out others' suffering as the limbs of their delight. They may look for insecurities in others so that they can be the Great Wise Teacher who fixes them. I once heard someone say, "The biggest trip of the guru is playing on people's insecurities." I thought that was an incredibly sharp point. If one becomes a teacher, the point is to benefit others, not inflate one's pride. Without a clearly established good motivation, it is easy to let teaching turn into an ego trip.

In recent years, dharma has gotten quite popular in the West. You can go to the grocery store and find magazines with articles on meditation or pictures of His Holiness the Dalai Lama. And I think the popularity of the dharma will keep increasing. This trend has given many people ideas about profiting from the dharma, often as teachers. Sometimes they have the sincere intention to benefit others. But if you want to become a teacher and don't examine that drive deeply, there's a good chance that your motivation will be tainted by self-centered goals, such as power, influence, respect, or money.

I've noticed that when people start going down this track, their progress ends. Before they had the idea of becoming teachers, they studied the dharma sincerely and humbly, intending to make an impression on their own mind. But once they get on the teaching track, their objective changes to explaining their knowledge to other people. When instructing others becomes the focus, they stop contemplating deeply. They stop taking the dharma to heart and seeing how it applies to their own lives. Once that happens, no amount of study and practice will propel them further along the path of enlightenment. They become immune to the dharma, too jaded for anything profound to get through. Therefore, as Patrul Rinpoche says in *Words of My Perfect Teacher,* "Do not take these instructions as a window through which to observe others' faults, but rather as a mirror for examining your own."

Point Seven

Guidelines for Mind Training

We are now at the final point, the guidelines for mind training. Compared to the "commitments" from the previous point, these pieces of advice are a little more relaxed. They are considered additional supports to help us live and practice in accord with the spirit of lojong.

39. Use one practice for everything.

Since intention is the driving force behind every achievement in the world, when we set out on the bodhisattva's path we should set the highest possible intention. Otherwise the outcome of our practice will be limited; there will not be any force to take it further than where we aimed. Therefore, our intention should be to completely let go of self-importance by working for the ultimate benefit of others.

It is a noble intention to wish others temporary pleasure and freedom from pain. But those states, even if they last an entire lifetime, will come to an end. They are unreliable. So the motivation behind our practice should be to bring all sentient beings to ultimate, irreversible happiness and ultimate, irreversible freedom from suffering and its causes. Our aim is to bring all sentient beings, who have been our mothers, to complete enlightenment.

As I said in the sixth point, we should value this kind of visionary love over a love that is based on transient emotions. However euphoric or explosive our emotions may be, if they don't last, what good will they do our mother sentient beings? Bodhisattvas do enjoy the powerful emotions of love and compassion, but their focus is on a deep and long-lasting commitment to keep working for others until the job is done. Without such a stable commitment, our efforts are likely to be based on our moods. When we're in a good mood, we have bodhicitta; when we're not, we don't. The attitude of the bodhisattvas is more mature. It gives them the patience to see things through all the way to the end. With visionary love, we can stay on track without easily becoming discouraged or giving up.

Therefore, whether we are on our meditation cushion or out in the world, we should always be looking at our motivation. If it is joined with visionary love, then all our activities in life will naturally become oriented toward helping others. It will be as natural as a swan gliding into a lake. The swan needs no encouragement to swim because swimming brings it contentment. When we have the yearning and commitment to bring ultimate benefit to others, then everything we do will bring us contentment because it will be connected to our deepest aspiration. Everything we encounter, even hardships, will increase our wisdom, compassion, and ability to benefit others.

In this way, we will make natural and inevitable progress and be sure to reach enlightenment sooner than later. If we progress even one percent of the way to enlightenment in this lifetime, then in one hundred lifetimes we will be equal to the Buddha himself. One hundred lifetimes may seem like a long time, but it is nothing when compared with the countless eons we have been in samsara. And these hundred lifetimes will not be like our other lives wandering aimlessly from one form of self-importance to another. As we continually let go of our small self, we will find ourselves going from joy to greater joy.

40. Use a single corrective for everything.

Having established the ultimate motivation of bodhicitta, we must always be vigilant about whether we are losing our yearning and commitment to help others. We may feel inspired to dedicate ourselves wholeheartedly to our altruistic vision, but then find ourselves beset by obstacles. Various conditions of our life may fall apart. Important relationships may become more difficult. We may be treated unjustly or falsely accused. Or the obstacles may come from the inside. Suddenly we are in the grip of powerful, self-centered emotions. It may seem like our self-clinging has gotten worse since we started practicing lojong. We start to think, "Maybe this is too difficult. Maybe this is beyond my capabilities and limits. Maybe this isn't right for me."

If you find this happening to you, if you find your visionary love is getting lost among your difficulties, then examine where this track is headed. What will you be like if your bodhicitta disappears? Won't you be more closed down? More disconnected from the world and from your own good heart? Is that the direction you want to go?

When we examine in this way, we realize we have no choice but to triumph over our obstacles. Our heart needs to triumph, because if it doesn't, we will be back in our ordinary state of self-importance. We may even end up worse off than before because we will carry a sense of failure about not fulfilling our bodhisattva vision. When we feel deeply discouraged to the point of wanting to give up, we need to realize that our mind is in a dangerous situation. Whatever happens, we cannot give up our bodhicitta. There is far too much at stake.

If certain people are treating us badly, we can choose not to be in their proximity for the time being. We can create some space. But we cannot let anyone ruin us as bodhisattvas. This may sound harsh, but if we lose our care—even for a single individual—then we are losing our commitment to attain enlightenment for the benefit of all mother sentient beings. Whenever we stop caring for one person, we are giving in to the ignorant demands of our tyrannical small self. We are forgetting that everyone wants to be happy and free from suffering just as much as we do. Instead we are just focusing on our hurt ego. Doing so is not in our best interest. When we indulge our self-importance, we strengthen it.

In order to maintain our long-term commitment, we need skillful methods to tolerate emotional pain. Again, I want to emphasize that this doesn't mean being hard on ourselves, or thinking we have failed when we feel angry. Nor is this an attitude of "grin and bear it." We can use gentle methods such as sitting on our cushion and practicing tonglen.

For example, we can think, "Because of my own self-centered past actions I have harmed others. This has led to their harming me in this life. Right now, how many beings are suffering as a result of their karma in this very way? How many beings are sowing seeds for their own future suffering by indulging in ego-oriented behavior? How many beings who are now causing harm have no idea about karma, and will keep destroying themselves with their own actions indefinitely? And how many aspiring bodhisattvas, even those who have learned about karma, have been discouraged by their obstacles just as I have been? May I take all these beings' suffering, harmful tendencies, and ignorant thoughts upon myself. May the pain I am going through burn up the pain of all other beings. May I offer them all my good fortune, understanding of dharma, and positive thoughts. In doing so, may all beings, myself and others, become free of all suffering and its causes."

41. Two things to do: one at the beginning, one at the end.

When you wake up in the morning, don't just jump out of bed with a lot of anxiety in your heart and reach for your coffee or get in the shower. Take a moment to think to yourself, "How am I going to spend this day? How am I going to work on reducing my self-importance? How can I work toward fulfilling my vision to benefit others?" Cultivate a deep longing to become a bodhisattva.

Without setting a clear intention for the day, it's difficult to have a greater purpose than merely cherishing and protecting the small self. I find it helpful to first put things into perspective by thinking about how countless beings throughout the universe are suffering. That gives me a better idea of how much needs to be done. It's not as if I can do it all in a day, or a year, or even a lifetime. Today I will do what I can to benefit the few beings in my world. But I will also keep in mind the vast number of beings in samsara, who I can only reach through prayers and through practices such as tonglen. And as I continue to train my mind in bodhicitta, my ability to benefit more beings—and benefit them more profoundly—will keep increasing.

Having this kind of perspective prevents us from being overly anxious about helping those within our reach. If we become fixated on the few around us, such as our family and friends, then there is a danger of this group becoming just a slightly larger version of the small self. This failure to see the bigger picture may merely end up increasing our attachment, aggression, and confusion.

At the end of the day, don't just conk out with exhaustion or put yourself to sleep with alcohol. First, take a little time to review your day. Ask yourself, "How did I spend my time? What was my mind like? How did my interactions with others go? Was I focused more on myself or on others? Did I meet the intentions I set in the morning? Did I do well as a bodhisattva?" If you did well in your actions and your mind was full of bodhicitta, then rejoice and dedicate the merit of your good day for the enlightenment of all beings.

If you had a negative mind-set throughout the day and did things you regret, don't be down on yourself. Take the opportunity to see what role self-importance played in your actions. Use this as a reminder that everything you don't want in life comes from your attachment to the small self. Acknowledge the need to go deeper into the lojong teachings and put them into practice. Instead of berating yourself for your failure, make a simple confession, and then let it go. Make a joyful aspiration to do better the next day, and then go to sleep. If you let your regrets go instead of chewing on them, you will be able to sleep well.

42. Whichever of the two arises, be patient.

Two things happen in our lives. We experience pain and suffering, or we experience joy and happiness. Both of these come from previous karma, whether from past lives or much more recently. Both can equally derail us from the path of dharma.

When suffering comes, we should realize that it is the inevitable result of self-importance and all its aftereffects, from the five poisons to the negative actions they lead us into. Without self-importance, there is no reason we would experience any pain. If that isn't clear to us, we should spend more time analyzing the mechanism of our suffering, according to the way that is described in these lojong teachings.

Once we acknowledge that self-importance is at the root of our pain, we need to rouse the courage to take responsibility for our own suffering and put it to good use. It will do no good to indulge in "poor me." Though a bit of self-pity is natural, if we don't shake it off, we may find ourselves drowning in it. No one, not even the most sympathetic and soothing friend, can prevent this from happening to us. Our only choice is to pick ourselves up and work with our minds. If we look for some remedy outside of mind training, we will be missing the target. Any method that doesn't address our self-importance will be nothing more than a distraction.

A more effective way of dealing with our suffering is to look around and realize that this is just how it is for beings like ourselves who are in samsara. Think about what it might be like to be in a war, a famine, or an epidemic. Think about the pain that most animals go through, whether domesticated or in the wild. At this moment, many beings are going through such intense suffering that we can't even imagine what it would be like to be in their place. Taking the time to think about the suffering of others has the twofold benefit of making us appreciate our own situation and of increasing our compassion. Instead of getting caught in resentment or depression, we can use our misfortunes as opportunities to practice tonglen.

For many practitioners, however, suffering is less of an obstacle than happiness. When they feel pain and sorrow, they spend a lot of time on the cushion, working with their mind, practicing lojong. But when things go well, that's a whole different story. How can happiness turn into an obstacle and what should we do when that occurs?

When good things happen in our life, it can feel like being on vacation in Hawaii or the Bahamas. We think, "Things are going so well. I *have to* enjoy this. I can't ignore what's happening here. How could I isolate myself in practice mode?" A kind of party mentality takes over, often just at the time that our practice has started to go well. When our mind gets high and excited, our determination to be free of samsara tends to go out the window. We lose the wider perspective that we have worked so hard to cultivate. You can be sure that when good circumstances influence you in this way, you are under the spell of obstacles. A similar problem occurs when your lojong is going well and the lover you have always wanted walks through your door. Or maybe your investment suddenly bears fruit. Or you become famous overnight. If you take your good fortune and just party with it, your practice will go down, down, down. You will become a loafer, wasting your time and letting the strength of your mind wear out completely. You will not be inclined to put your head into the doorway of a dharma center or even sit on your cushion at home. To self-reflect or meditate in the midst of your party will seem very unappealing.

Positive circumstances coming into our lives tend to make us excited. Western people usually equate excitement with happiness. In the East, at least traditionally, excitement is not considered a sign of well-being. When we are excited, our energy is unsettled. Our mind loses its clarity and therefore its strength and its poise. Because we are preoccupied with our excited feelings, we forget about our most important aspirations. Our mindfulness and vigilant introspection take a holiday, which puts us in danger of falling for the many traps set by our self-importance. Until the energy of excitement dies down, we are derailed from the path of dharma. Excitement is sometimes our ego's last attempt to hold us captive. When we are moving nicely forward, we suddenly become excited, and our progress in bodhicitta seems less significant. We forget to honor what's most important in our lives. But inevitably, excitement leads to a crash. We then have to face what has happened while our minds were away.

Therefore, when we encounter good fortune, we should do our best not to get overly excited, cocky, or arrogant. We should remember where our good fortune has come from: thoughts and actions based on care for other sentient beings. Instead of just trying to prolong our fortunate state, we should keep cultivating its causes. Otherwise our merit will be like a tree that bears fruit once and then dies. We should keep generating bodhicitta and letting go of our attachment to the small self. It may seem like our self-centered activities are what have brought about the positive events in our life, but this is just ego doing what it likes to do: claiming credit where it is undeserved. When we acknowledge the true source of happiness, our excitement can calm down and we can get on with the process of continuing our bodhisattva path, while enjoying the fruits of our past positive deeds. If we have good health, we can use our strength and energy to practice. If we have wealth or a high position, we can use those advantages to help others. Whatever good we encounter, we can make prayers that other beings also be endowed with such positive circumstances—minus the excitement.

43. Protect the two as dearly as your life.

The "two" here are the general commitments and guidelines of dharma and the specific commitments and guidelines of lojong. When the slogan says to protect these as dearly as your life, it's not like someone is putting a gun to your head and making you choose between your life and lojong. It's more an encouragement to talk to yourself about priorities.

We have lived countless lives in samsara and will live countless more of these lives in the future. What has this infinite series of lives amounted to so far? Have they led to our enlightenment? No. On the contrary, we have remained stuck in the same pattern of self-importance leading to self-centered emotions, leading to all varieties and intensities of suffering, both for ourselves and others. Now we finally have access to the wisdom and methods that can lead us out of this trap.

From this point of view, nothing—not even our dear life—merits more honor and appreciation than the dharma. Of course we hold our life very dear, but without a path leading away from self-importance, how valuable is this life, really? We are strongly attached to it, but our attachment alone doesn't imbue an ego-based life with any true value. But when this life is joined with dharma, with lojong, with the exchange of self and other, it becomes a vehicle to take us far along the path to enlightenment.

If we value these teachings so highly, we will always be thinking about how we can make the best use of them. We will appreciate the stark contrast between our two choices: to walk courageously on the bodhisattva's path, or to fall back into the clutches of the small self. We will become determined not to let anything prevent us from opening our hearts to the vast universe of our mother sentient beings.

44. Train in the three difficulties.

When self-centered emotions such as attachment and anger arise in our minds, it is difficult to see them as "negative." We usually take them to be normal. Though we suffer as a result of these neuroses, we don't necessarily connect the emotion and the suffering as cause and effect. Nor do we look into the source of the emotion, the tendency to cherish and protect the small self. Either we don't know how to make these connections, or we are in denial and don't want to make them.

In either case, we need to purposely train in recognizing how disturbing emotions are responsible for our suffering. This doesn't mean just assuming that anger, for example, is *bad*. It means getting to know how anger brings us suffering, through firsthand experience and self-reflection. Only this approach will lead to a genuine longing to be free of these emotions.

Training in this first "difficulty" of recognition requires mindfulness and vigilant introspection. It is like establishing an intelligence agency in our mind, to protect us from the various threats of our archenemy, self-importance. We have to maintain vigilance with respect to our disturbing emotions, checking their activities and using wisdom to keep them from proliferating. This will spare us a great deal of suffering. But we also have to do this in a healthy way, without suppression or self-disparagement. We should see our neuroses not as *my* neuroses, but as universal experiences—the inevitable results of the confusion and ignorance that come from clinging to the small self.

Once we recognize what is happening, we can practice the second difficulty, transforming our disturbing emotions by applying the appropriate remedy. For working with your self-centered emotions, the lojong teachings are full of effective practices, such as tonglen. Study these remedies in all their subtleties, experience their beneficial effects, gain confidence in them, and make them part of your repertoire for working with neuroses when they arise. Then, once you know the traditional wisdom and methods well, you can be creative. But I recommend that you first learn and understand the tried and true ways, so you don't add to the confusion by inadvertently creating "remedies" that increase your self-importance.

The third difficulty is consistently practicing until the disturbing emotions no longer arise. This requires a lot of time, effort, and enthusiasm. But it is within our reach. All the buddhas of the past have accomplished this, and the essence of our minds is no different from theirs. We must keep practicing until our minds are completely united with the wisdom of the lojong. With the practices of relative bodhicitta, we can purify the small self and embrace the universal self of all sentient beings. Then, when we are ready to practice absolute bodhicitta, we can completely uproot our ignorant belief in the reality of our self and our world. Since this ignorance is the basis for all our self-centered emotions to arise, when we go beyond it, our neuroses will be deprived of their birthplace.

45. Take up the three principal causes.

The first cause of progressing on the path to enlightenment is having a spiritual friend. In the dharma, we can't accomplish our deepest aspirations completely on our own. Our self-importance is too troublesome and tricky to allow that to happen. That is why it said "Without the spiritual friend, there is no mention of Buddha." A spiritual friend is a living human being who can explain the teachings and practices to you and who can help your understanding gradually unfold. This teacher should be someone who inspires great confidence in you, based on his or her realization of the deepest meaning of the teachings. If the teacher only speaks the words of the teachings but doesn't embody them to the core, then expecting to make progress by following him or her will be like expecting a beautiful form to come out of an inferior mold.

The second cause is a workable mind. In order for the teachings to shape us, our mind must be made of material that can be shaped—more like clay than rock. We have to be open to being transformed. If we study the dharma just to acquire some new concepts but are not interested in integrating the teachings into our lives, then we will never change for the better.

A lot of people fear being open in this way, equating it with gullibility. If this is how we feel, then we should think about the great practitioners of the past. Were they naïve and simple-minded? On the contrary, they were highly intelligent, refined people. But seeing the relative merits of being open versus being shut down, they chose to be more like clay than like rock. Mipham Rinpoche, one of the greatest teachers and scholars in the history of Tibet, had very few disciples. When people asked him to be their teacher, he would ask, "Are you easy to work with?" If they said no, then he would decline their request, saying, "I can only accept a disciple who is willing to transform."

The third cause is conducive conditions in your life. These include food, clothing, and a supportive environment. Although the lojong teachings can be applied to any situation, even the most difficult, we should still work on creating supportive conditions for study and practice. For example, if you make the choice to live near your spiritual friend or at a dharma center, or if you choose to spend your free time in a practice situation rather than doing something mundane, then you are creating causes to make significant progress on your path.

If we have all three causes in our lives, it's important to appreciate and cherish them, rather than take them for granted. It's easy to take things for granted, even if we don't intend to do so. To counteract this tendency, we should actively contemplate our good fortune and strive to make the most out of it in order to develop our bodhicitta. We should think about the vast majority of beings who don't have these conditions, and then practice tonglen, mentally taking on their suffering and giving them whatever we have. And if we are missing any of these three causes, we should also think about the countless beings who don't have them. We can pray that we and all others gain the three causes, and again we can take this opportunity to practice tonglen.

46. Practice to not let the three degenerate.

When we have a spiritual friend in our lives, we should take care not to let this invaluable connection degenerate. We especially need to maintain two aspects of our relation to the teacher: yearning and respect. We yearn to embrace the teachings and the path fully until our bodhicitta becomes as deep as our teacher's. And when we acknowledge the profound benefit that the teacher brings to our lives, we feel immense respect.

According to the theory of evolution, human beings have evolved from single-celled organisms over billions of years. But now that we have human bodies, we have to keep evolving until we attain enlightenment. This is our basic disposition, and it will come to fruition at some point, sooner than later, we hope. Animals know how to find food and shelter, how to take care of themselves and their young. If that is all we do with our human lives, then how can we claim to be more evolved than animals? Having a spiritual friend puts us at the doorstep of completing our evolution, but we must be careful never to let our yearning and respect decline.

Next, we need to maintain our enthusiasm for practice. During painful periods of our lives, we may feel disheartened and lose our former cheerfulness about lojong. But we can always practice the exchange of self and other, and this practice works. When things seem hopeless, this is the light at the end of the tunnel. It helps us transform self-centeredness into altruism, pain and suffering into joy and peace.

I had a student who passed away in her late eighties. A few years before she died, she had to move to a nursing home. This is how she described it to me: "We wake up and we wait for breakfast. Then we have breakfast and we wait for lunch. Then we have lunch and we wait for dinner. Then we have dinner and we wait to go to bed. Then we go to bed and we wait till the morning. Without the dharma, my life would be very depressing. But with the dharma, it's OK." I thought she was a great example of someone who didn't let her enthusiasm degenerate.

Finally, we should take care to keep all our commitments in the dharma and not fall into shamelessness. Essentially, we need to maintain a clear sense of what actions are right and wrong. This should not be based on religious ideas but decency. The true measure of our decency is how much we are focused on others and how much on our small self. When we maintain mindfulness and vigilant introspection, we remain free of any cause for embarrassment.

47. Remain inseparable from the three.

These "three" are our body, speech, and mind, the three means by which we create positive and negative karma. We should try our best not to let our mindfulness drift away from these three doors. Instead, we should employ them all with purposeful intention.

We can use our body to take care of others' physical needs. We can save the lives of animals who are soon to be killed, such as worms or lobsters. We can make offerings. If we live near a dharma center, we can help with building, cleaning, or running errands. With our speech, we can share the dharma or comfort people who are suffering. We can recite prayers, such as "May all sentient beings enjoy happiness and the root of happiness." There are countless ways to use our body and speech for greater purposes than cherishing the small self.

But since our actions of body and speech originate in our mind, what we do with our mind is the most important. This comes down to the main point of the lojong: transforming our attitude from self-centeredness to altruism. If we continually train in practices such as tonglen, if we steep our minds in bodhicitta, then all our actions of body, speech, and mind will naturally bring more and more benefit to the world we live in.

48. Practice impartially toward everything. Deep and comprehensive mastery overall is essential.

Because of our attachment to the small self, some beings are easier than others to bring into our lojong practice. So we should work on making our practice more inclusive. For example, if we start with our dearest friends and family members, we should eventually expand our practice to include everyone we encounter. Then the next step would be to include all sentient beings, near or far.

It's funny, however, that we often need the greatest patience not with our "enemies," but with those closest to us. Even if they aren't threatening or harming us at all, we often feel our irritation rising up. Our familiarity makes us less tolerant. In the West, familiarity is often equated with friendliness, and politeness is often understood as being cold. But this is not the case in the lojong. When we're too familiar with people, we tend to take them for granted, or even take advantage of them. When we're too casual, a lot of negativity can come out, especially through our mouths. So I would suggest being polite, not just with strangers, but with the people we know best and live closest to.

49. Always meditate on whatever is most challenging.

To practice the dharma successfully, we think we need a quiet, soothing environment with nobody bothering us. This may be true for some practices, but it's not a requirement for lojong. In fact, "obstacles" are often the greatest aids to overcoming self-importance. We can make more rapid progress by bearing with difficulties than by living in too much comfort and serenity.

This is why Atisha, the teacher who brought the lojong teachings to Tibet, liked to travel around with an irritating tea boy who could pop his bubble if he ever got complacent. Most of us, however, don't have to recruit a tea boy; we can practice with whoever is in our space. Whoever we find difficult to work with on a daily basis—our children, our spouse, our roommates, our in-laws—can provide us with ample opportunity to practice lojong. Instead of thinking that our lack of space is an inconvenience, we can take advantage of having to rub skins with the people close to us.

Furthermore, if someone you've always been kind to turns against you, that is an even more precious challenge. You may feel that their behavior is unfair, that it goes against your ideas about how things should work. But remember that nothing happens outside of the law of cause and effect. You are experiencing the effects of clinging to the small self, and now you have a chance to work with that clinging. In the lojong, whatever provokes your mind the most is also the greatest opportunity.

50. Do not rely on other factors.

Being able to apply the lojong doesn't depend on external conditions. We can practice in both favorable and unfavorable circumstances. When we are in transition, when our lives are chaotic, when we go through upheaval and stress, we often find ourselves practicing less. We may have less time to spend on the cushion, but even so, lojong is always available. We don't need special conditions in order to work on our self-importance. If we make it our life's work to step out of the small self, then we can practice lojong no matter what happens. But if we're not interested in remedying our self-centeredness, then it doesn't matter how favorable our outer life seems to be. We will not be able to practice meaningfully.

51. Practice what is essential now.

We have endured suffering for countless eons in samsara, having taken innumerable forms of sentient life. But we are still where we always have been: in samsara. Now we finally have the teachings and practices that can liberate us from samsara once and for all. In order to take advantage of this opportunity, we have to feel the preciousness of it, and not let our minds be taken over by meaningless pursuits. But this slogan doesn't suggest that we artificially suppress our desires. It is rather a call to recognize our good fortune and feel inspired to make the most of it.

One of the greatest aspects of human intelligence is that we can make long-term plans. Of all the possible long-term plans, which one is supreme? It is the plan to become enlightened. We should pursue the dharma with this plan in mind, rather than as a chore, or for any other pathetic reason. And we should follow this path, not merely to free ourselves from suffering, but to bring all our mother sentient beings to complete enlightenment.

On this path, we can emphasize study or practice. Study is important, but practice is even more so. Of all practices, there is nothing higher than the practice of bodhicitta. The most powerful way of practicing bodhicitta is by following the teacher's instructions. And of all the ways to do this, the best is on the cushion. As one of Chekawa Yeshe Dorje's teachers said to him, "I've always found all my answers on my meditation cushion." If we arrange our priorities according to this slogan, then we will surely make the most of our opportunity.

52. Do not dwell in misunderstanding.

This slogan addresses six positive qualities that we try to cultivate, and how they can be mistakenly co-opted by the small self.

The first misunderstanding is *mistaken patience*. When we have to endure difficulties in the study and practice of dharma, we don't reflect on how much this will purify our minds and bring benefit to ourselves and others. We think, "This is too damn difficult. No one else in my entire family or town works this hard." But when we hear of people getting up at five in the morning, working four stressful jobs, and then coming home at ten at night, we think, "Oh, it's so great that he or she is working so hard. That is life!"

How much physical labor and worry does a farmer endure just to end up with a little bit of rice at the end of the year? How many years of study and hardship do people go through to get good jobs and promotions? But in the end they don't really get anything more significant than the ability to buy food and clothing. In samsara, we go through so much for such little gain. Yet it seems normal to tolerate these mundane hardships and abnormal to face challenges in the dharma that will benefit us profoundly, for life after life.

The next misunderstanding is *mistaken aspiration*. We have the knowledge and good sense to see how stepping out of our small self and directing our care to other beings would relieve us from our painful, self-centered emotions, and enable us to benefit others immensely. We have practices, such as the exchange of self and other, that have been proven to bring about this transformation effectively. But somehow we don't have much enthusiasm for lojong. On the other hand, if our friend gets into a good relationship or gains some recognition, we get so excited and say things like, "Finally, this little bird has made it into the world!"

If we get the right job or become famous, we become so thrilled, as if we are on top of the world. But when we have a chance to free ourselves forever from the intense suffering of samsara, a chance that is incalculably rare, we don't feel very motivated to take advantage of the opportunity. We are more interested in aspiring for short-term gain than for enlightenment. So we waste our lives in vain.

There's a saying that the dharma practitioner's life is always difficult and challenging in the beginning. But as it goes on, it gets easier and easier, better and better. Conventional life tends to be the opposite. It may start off easier and happier, but as time goes on it gets harder. The conventional person ends up in a place of loss and disappointment, whereas the practitioner ends up in a place of ease. When we have the opportunity to be a genuine practitioner, but instead use our minds to yearn for better outward conditions, such as more money or comfort, then we are misdirecting our aspirations.

Mistaken taste refers to desiring all the pleasurable things in samsara. Our desires generally come from a painful feeling of lacking something. But samsaric pleasure—such as what we get from our accomplishments or our lifestyle—is like a patch that only temporarily relieves the pain of lacking.

It's hard enough to get what we want in samsara; many things have to fall into place, which may or may not happen. But even if we do get what we want, how long do we experience satisfaction? Not very long. Instead of enjoying our fulfilled desires, we keep finding new things to crave, which only perpetuates our dissatisfaction. We become addicted to the futile pursuit of applying new patches. Shantideva compares samsaric craving to licking honey from a razor blade. Because we are addicted to the sweet taste, we keep licking the blade, cutting our tongue over and over again. We crave the sweetness so much that we can't make the connection to the pain that follows. Instead of following these meaningless drives, we would be better off cultivating a taste for the delicious nectar of dharma.

Next we have *mistaken compassion*. We don't realize how much ordinary human beings, people just like ourselves, suffer. How many different painful experiences does the average person go through in one lifetime, from birth to death? And compared to ourselves, who are relatively fortunate, the vast majority of beings in samsara have it much worse. The mere fact of being alive and having a sensitive mind implies tremendous ongoing suffering. But we are either not aware of this, or we see it as just the way things are, no big deal. Even if someone appears to be doing well in this life, that happiness is only a fleeting experience caused by some positive actions in the past. If it isn't sustained by the practice of bodhicitta, then habitual self-importance will again bring the person back to the realm of suffering.

We don't usually have much compassion for the ordinary tragedy of samsara, but when we see someone enduring hardships to pursue the dharma, we feel shocked, overwhelmed, afraid. Milarepa, the eleventh-century yogi whose life story is the most popular narrative in Tibet, went through many harsh trials on his spiritual path. When we hear stories about him subsisting on nettles and living in the snowy mountains with only a piece of cotton to wear, we tend to feel sorry for him. But as the saying goes, "Ordinary beings see Milarepa as crazy, but Milarepa sees ordinary beings as crazy." By going through his hardships, Milarepa dissolved his attachment to the small self and attained enlightenment—the ultimate happiness and freedom from suffering—in one lifetime. But we sentient beings, in order merely to survive, go through our own excruciating hardships, which bring us no closer to liberation from our tyrannical self-importance. So who deserves compassion more?

When we are in the position to support or influence people, we should be mindful of the direction we encourage them to follow. Encouraging someone to go after ordinary, self-centered aims, but not encouraging them to practice the dharma, is *mistaken care*. For example, we may think it is in our child's best interest to have a successful career, start a family, and get nicely settled in samsara. But if our child's actions are motivated only by self-importance, these pursuits will not lead to any happiness whatsoever. On the other hand, if we influence our children to practice the dharma and we support them in their path, then we are putting effort into something that will pay off. The eventual result will be enlightenment, which will bring immense benefit not just to one person, but to countless other sentient beings.

The last misunderstanding is *mistaken joy*. Even though we have set out on the path of altruism, recognizing the great benefits of exchanging self and other, our self-importance still makes it hard to rejoice when others do well. Instead we may find ourselves feeling joyful and satisfied when bad things happen to certain people. Hearing news about others going downhill may make us feel delighted.

If we have this unwholesome tendency, we should take some time to consider the advantages of being able to rejoice in others' happiness. When we can really enjoy the good fortune of others, we always have abundant causes for happiness in our own mind. We can always think of people who are rich, famous, beautiful, intelligent, talented, successful, or have any other qualities we desire for ourselves. Best of all, we can rejoice in the accomplishments of the buddhas and bodhisattvas, or anyone who is finding joy and freedom for the benefit of others through the practice of lojong.

53. Do not be sporadic.

We tend to go back and forth in our priorities. Sometimes we focus on accomplishing our spiritual goals, devoting many hours a day and feeling very committed. Other times we get caught up in the ambitions of the conventional world and don't even have the intention to practice. This kind of inconsistency undermines our self-confidence and prevents us from making any progress.

Sometimes we may fall into self-satisfaction. This is never an appropriate attitude for lojong. If we are complacent about our path, we will never do what it takes to drive the tenacious rascal of self-importance out of our hearts. This slogan urges us not to check out. There is no such thing as a vacation from working with our mind. We should continually contemplate how we can go deeper in our practice. Mind training requires nothing external, not even a cushion. All we need is a mind, and that we always have.

54. Train wholeheartedly.

Unless we're fully committed to the lojong, we won't succeed in eradicating our self-importance. This slogan encourages us to make this commitment, rather than merely testing the lojong to see if it works.

To avoid practicing with a half-hearted, second-guessing attitude, we need to understand what we're doing. As my teacher Dilgo Khyentse Rinpoche often used to say, "It's important to practice, but first you need to learn *how* to practice." Learning how to practice gives us the confidence to do it wholeheartedly. If we understand the benefits of lojong, if we know how it works, if we grasp the relationship between the practice and our own mind, and if we trust in its effectiveness, then we will naturally train wholeheartedly. We will naturally train to become bodhisattvas the way that athletes train for the Olympics. On the outer level, we will exert ourselves, and on the inner level, which is even more important, our mind will be completely in sync with the lojong.

55. Find liberation through both reflection and analysis.

Our minds have two related abilities: to look at things in general and to examine details. In Tibetan these are called *tokpa* and *chöpa*. The first is like identifying a forest; the second is like examining the trees in that forest.

We should apply these faculties to understand our disturbing emotions. For example, if you notice that you feel upset, you can ask: *Why do I feel upset?* Because I have been insulted. *What was said that made me feel so insulted? Why did that insult me, when it didn't insult my friend?* Examine the situation from all angles: from your point of view, from the other's point of view, from the dharmic view, from the worldly view, in relation to the past, present, and future. Learn everything there is to know about the subject and get to the bottom of it. Once the light of your critical intelligence fully shines, it will be easy to free yourself by applying the lojong practices such as tonglen.

It's important to do this practice systematically, going from general to specific, without skipping around. If you jump from one general theme to another, or from one detail to another, then you won't learn much. You will be dwelling in vagueness. This process requires effort and may take you out of your comfort zone. But it is a process you can master, whether you're an intellectual or an artist, whether you're educated or uneducated. It's a matter of using your innate emotional intelligence to understand your own experience.

Learning how to apply these two mental faculties will make you feel confident and self-reliant. You will be able to understand the mind deeply from your own experience. In this way you will become a great teacher to yourself as well as a benefit to others.

56. Do not feel the world owes you.

If you are training your mind in letting go of the small self, and you are serving others in your outer actions, don't have the attitude that the world has a debt to pay you. Don't start thinking that everyone should respect you for being so special and magnificent. Feeding your self-importance in that way would be anti-lojong.

We should remember why we are on this path and how it will lead us to the ultimate joy of enlightenment. Shifting our affection from our ego to other beings will ultimately free us from all the sufferings of samsara. Why should we get puffed up about being so good to ourselves?

57. Do not be reactive.

Sometimes we are feeling so hypersensitive, it's as if our mind is covered with blisters. When something painful happens to us, we immediately collapse into depression, as if our spirit has been broken forever. This slogan encourages us to have more poise in our mind. Before our overreaction spills out, we should first try to work with the experience from within.

We never suffer without cause. All negative circumstances come about because of our own past negative actions, which in turn come from our self-centered emotions, such as attachment and aggression. And the source of all of this pain is our own self-importance. If we get worked up about the result without looking into its cause, aren't we being a little superficial? Instead of reacting so strongly to whatever happens to us, we can take the opportunity to purify the root of the problem by practicing the exchange of self and other.

58. Do not be temperamental.

Our emotional ups and downs can create great waves of disturbance in our environment. If we experience a lot of mood swings and, on top of that, we express our emotions to the world at maximum volume, then people will not want to be around us.

Think about what it feels like to be around a temperamental person, someone who's pleased one moment and upset the next, laughing one moment and crying the next. It is hard to find any peace around these people. Everything you say or do, everyone whose name you mention, could provoke a whole stream of comments, attitudes, and emotions.

There is nothing wrong with having strong emotions come up. We can't control what arises in our mind. An emotion such as anger isn't "bad." But if our reactions to what arises cause us to disturb other people and our environment, then we should at least be interested in working with our mind.

This is especially important in relationships between spouses or partners. When one or both parties become temperamental, communication breaks down. The members of the couple feel they can't talk openly, so they withdraw and keep their discomfort suppressed inside. Then one or both of the people may end up doing deceitful things on their own. I'm not, however, suggesting that couples do a lot of "processing." Having to process everything could become another neurotic way of being together. With lojong, we always try to focus on working things out in our own mind first. Then, when we have become more even-tempered and less worked up, we will be much easier to get along with.

59. Do not self-aggrandize.

As Shantideva said, "When you treat yourself to a good meal, you don't expect yourself to thank yourself." Letting go of the small self and being kind and compassionate to others is like treating yourself to the most excellent meal. It is its own reward.

Whenever we practice dharma, we should let go of any expectations of praise or renown. Whenever we do anything to benefit others, we should do it without strings attached. Otherwise we are setting ourselves up for disappointment. If we don't work with our habit of attaching strings, we will eventually become disillusioned with the practice of bodhicitta. Being generous, opening our heart, following a spiritual friend, falling in love—these will start seeming like naïve and stupid things to do. We will become hard inside and eventually turn into grumpy old men and grumpy old ladies.

Because of our long history of self-importance, our habit of attaching strings runs very deep. Often we are not even aware of our expectations. Therefore, whenever we do anything for others, it is wise to remind ourselves of what Shantideva said about treating yourself to a good meal. Kindness and compassion naturally bring us peace of mind, so why nullify that peace by getting all worked up about our unmet expectations?

When we stop expecting anything from anyone else, we won't be so neurotically entangled with others. Because we are no longer invested in others' reactions, we will have nothing to gain or lose and nothing to quarrel about. More and more often, we will find ourselves in a state of peace.

Conclusion

These days most of us have a lot of books. Some of them are very profound. We read them and connect to them, but all too often, when we close our books, the wisdom remains theoretical. We can know that contemplating impermanence helps us cut through our attachments, but then rearrange the furniture in our burning house. We can know that all phenomena are like a dream, but we still desire things that won't make us happy, or reject threats that can't actually harm us. We can know that all our suffering comes from self-importance, and that blaming others is pointless and deluded, but then blame others nonetheless. We leave the teachings in our knowledge bank, not pressing our brains enough to squeeze out the blessing that can touch us.

How can we integrate these teachings into our lives? I think that only happens when we are faced with challenges and respond to them in a new way, not according to habitual self-importance. In other words, we respond by applying the exchange of self and other. When tonglen becomes our familiar way of being, the entire path unfolds easily in front of us. This difficult modern age turns out to be the perfect setting for our spiritual practice, proving far more hospitable to our growth than past eras of idealized calm and simplicity. When we figure out for ourselves how to apply the wisdom of books to whatever difficult circumstances arise in life, then that wisdom becomes part of our mind. We become transformed. My hope for every reader—as well as for myself—is that we will apply these lojong teachings again and again until they become part of who we are.

At that point, we'll be able to help others profoundly, starting with those who are close to us, such as our parents, children, spouses, and partners. We can help them first with our example, then, if they are open, with some words, and if they are even more open, with explicit guidance. We can be a small lamp that illuminates the area around us. When we think about illumination, we tend to think of something more like the sun, which casts brilliant light on entire planets. With that kind of ambition, the thought of lighting a small area around us doesn't sound very meaningful or attractive. But the grassroots way of affecting our world is much more steady and reliable than having to be a big-shot bodhisattva. It avoids the ever-present risk of self-importance moving in and taking over the whole enterprise. Each lamp consistently shines with inextinguishable bodhicitta, rather than flaring up as the unmanageable fire of ego. One lamp helps illuminate a few others, which illuminate a few others, and so on, in wider and wider circles. This is an incredible outcome. And it is within our reach.

The Seven Points of Mahayana Mind Training

Translators' Introduction

"Examine my words like a goldsmith examines gold. Don't take my word just because it is my word." Dzigar Kongtrul Rinpoche often paraphrases this advice of the Buddha. Rinpoche's reference directly invites, encourages, and challenges students of the buddhadharma to make these teachings their own. Examining the Buddha's words, or the words of our teachers, requires the ongoing process of the Three Wisdoms: hearing, contemplating, and meditating. It is through this process that we engage ourselves in the path of genuine personal transformation.

Chekawa Yeshe Dorje's *Seven Points* and Jamgon Kongtrul Lodro Thaye's commentary, *The Seven Points of Mahayana Mind Training: A Guide to Benefit Those Embarking on the Authentic Path to Enlightenment,* are sparkling gold—worthy of our most discerning examination. We have come to see that the intention of this and all lojong texts is to serve as a practical guide to recognizing, seizing, and uprooting our manifold self-centered tendencies—with a healthy dose of humor. Since this is perhaps the slipperiest and most challenging aspect of our personal and spiritual growth, we need determination and openness to comprehend clearly each of Chekawa's and Jamgon Kongtrul's profound and illuminating words.

During the process of translating the *Seven Points* and Jamgon Kongtrul's commentary, Kongtrul Rinpoche encouraged us to think of our work as an exercise in deep personal understanding. Mining the accurate meaning of a text such as this certainly requires a subtle and delicate consideration of context, purpose, and application: basically, what it means to really practice these teachings at every twist and turn of life. So in this way we understand the words "Examine my words like a goldsmith examines gold" as applying to translation as well.

Throughout the process of translating this text, we've come to see that there is really no way of separating student from translator. Indeed, the Buddha's phrase itself seems to equate study and practice with translation and empowers all students of dharma as translators of sorts. Working with teachings such as these through the process of the Three Wisdoms makes the words authentic personal assimilations, makes them part of our being, as they are meant to be.

We would like to thank Ken McLeod for his translation of the slogans and Jamgon Kongtrul's commentary, *The Great Path of Awakening*, as well as the other wonderful translations of the *Seven Points*. These have held us to a very high standard, and we are so grateful for this indirect encouragement. This version from Vairochana's Legacy is meant only to supplement what has already been so proficiently and poetically translated.

Translation is a deep and personal journey, and we make aspirations that we may have the merit to continue our endeavors, both for our own understanding and in order to contribute in our small way to the transplantation of the dharma in the Western world. As the saying goes, the dharma has no owner, it belongs to whomever studies it and puts it into practice. We will strive to own it ourselves, and at the same time, may our efforts also support and protect the legacy of Tibet's, where the dharma has survived and flourished for hundreds and hundreds of years. We who have benefited so much from this legacy feel profoundly indebted to the effort and perseverance of all the illustrious beings of the Snow Land of Tibet.

Kongtrul Rinpoche has been there for us every step of the way to give clarification and explanation on certain challenging slogans or phrases. We are utterly indebted to our kind teacher for his years with us at Guna Institute in India, where we learned not only the skills of translation, but more important, how to think clearly and deeply, and how to bring the teachings into our own experience. With this, our first publication, we also would like to thank His Eminence Tai Situ Rinpoche for his encouragement and support, and for honoring us with the name Vairochana's Legacy. May all beings benefit.

—VAIROCHANA'S LEGACY

A Guide to Benefit Those Embarking on the Authentic Path to Enlightenment

GURU BUDDHA BODHISATTVA BHYONAMA

With undivided faith, I place upon the crown of my head,
The lotus feet of the Supreme Sage,
Who first set in motion the wheel of love,
Who triumphed completely in the two benefits.

To the greatly renowned sons of the Victorious One,
Who, seizing the heroic ship of compassion,
Liberate beings from the ocean of suffering.
To Manjushri, Avalokiteshvara, and the others, I bow down.

To the unsurpassable spiritual friend,
Who expounds the excellent path of emptiness and compassion,
The guide of all the Victorious Ones,
At the feet of my guru, I prostrate.

The single path traversed by the Conqueror and his sons,
Easy to comprehend and uncorrupted,
Blissful to practice and entered with enthusiasm,
It is profound, and thus buddhahood is achieved. This I shall
   explain.

In order to transmit the instructions on the *Seven Points of Mind Training*, which are exalted and excellent pith instructions for the cultivation of bodhicitta, I shall explain three points: the source of the transmission, the general need for mind training, and the actual instructions.

The Source of the Transmission

The glorious Lord Atisha studied at length under three masters: Ser-lingpa Dharmakirti, master of bodhicitta, who received the transmission through the oral instructions of the exalted mind of the King of Sages and his sons; Guru Dharmarakshita, who realized emptiness by relying upon love and compassion, and who actually gave flesh from his very own body; and the yogi Guru Maitreya, who was able to take directly upon himself the sufferings of others. By way of great commitment and effort, and due to perfect hearing, bodhicitta came to fill Atisha's mind. He arrived as a protector of Tibet, and although he had immeasurable dharma teachings to impart, he relied only upon the methods described here. Ku, Ngok, and Drom were his three principal disciples among the infinite students of the three lineages whom he established in purification and liberation. Moreover, Drom-ton Rinpoche was Avalokiteshvara in person. These three disciples, emanations of the three buddha families, spread the three traditions of teaching: the scriptural texts, the key instructions, and the pith instructions.

These teachings were transmitted individually by a series of great spiritual friends. The tradition of elucidation of the six treatises of the Kadampas fell upon the Gelukpas, the teachings on the key instructions of the four truths fell upon the Dakpo Kagyu, and both schools preserved the traditions of the pith instructions on the sixteen essences. Similarly, the renowned and precious Kadampa school holds the lord of teaching, the seven dharmas and deities: the four deities that adorn the body, the three baskets that adorn the speech, and the threefold training by which the mind is adorned. Though the limitless instructions of this precious Kagyu tradition dwell firmly within the sutra system, and are also in some ways connected to the mantra tradition, they all show only the path of the union of emptiness and compassion. Because this teaching is primarily within the realm of relative bodhicitta, most of the great ones who held this transmission have revealed the tradition of the exchange of self and other and its capacity to lead to complete liberation. Of the many and varying traditions of commentaries on this method, the seven points taught here have arisen from the tradition of instruction of Chekawa Yeshe Dorje.

The Need for Mind Training

There is no use to consider the futile happiness that results from birth in the higher realms of gods and humans. The enlightenment of shravakas and pratyekabuddhas can be attained; however, it is not the ultimate nirvana. Thus we must strive solely for the state of the complete and perfect buddha. There are no methods that lead to this attainment other than those that rely upon the two meditations: relative bodhicitta, which trains the mind in love and compassion, and absolute bodhicitta, in which the mind rests evenly in a state of non-conception, free from elaboration. Nagarjuna states:

> This world and I, we wish to attain
> Unsurpassable enlightenment.
> The root of this is bodhicitta,
> Steadfast as the King of Mountains,
> Compassion, which touches all ends of the earth,
> And primordial wisdom which is not subject to duality.

Furthermore, regardless of the merit and wisdom we may possess, the basis of entry into the Mahayana (such as the paramitas and non-abiding nirvana) remains solely the generation of bodhicitta, which arises out of love and compassion. Even when final buddhahood is attained, there is nothing to be done other than to work for the benefit of others with non-conceptual compassion. Authentic absolute bodhicitta will not arise in the mind streams of beginners. But relative bodhicitta, should they train in it, will surely be born. And with the development of relative bodhicitta, absolute bodhicitta is naturally realized.

For these various reasons we must persistently meditate on relative bodhicitta in the beginning if we are to achieve any meaningful results in cultivating bodhicitta. For those who wish for instruction with respect to this, the basic method for training is as Shantideva says:

> For those who desire swiftly
> To protect themselves and all others,
> Employ the excellent secret,
> Of exchanging oneself for others.

Accordingly, the meditative stages for exchanging self and other are explained below. Other approaches to mind training are mere elaborations.

The Actual Instructions

This third section has two parts: the actual teachings of this tradition and the additional instructions of the transmission lineage.

First, the main teachings of this lineage.

The Seven Points:
1. The preliminaries teach the foundation of dharma practice
2. The main practice: training in bodhicitta
3. Transforming adversity into the path of enlightenment
4. An explanation of the practices as a way of life
5. Measures of proficiency in mind training
6. Commitments of mind training
7. Guidelines for mind training

I. The Preliminaries Teach the Foundation of Dharma Practice
As for the first point:

1. First, train in the preliminaries.

In this there are two sections: the preliminaries of a meditation session and preliminary instructions.

A. The Preliminaries of a Meditation Session

First, at the beginning of every meditation session, imagine your root guru above your head seated on a lotus and moon seat. His body is radiant and his face is smiling. With non-referential compassion he considers all beings. Think that he is in essence the complete embodiment of all the root and lineage gurus.

With devotion and yearning, recite the lineage supplication if you like, and in particular, the following prayer a hundred or a thousand times.

Oh guru, great and utterly true spiritual friend, I pray that you will bless me. That you may inspire love, compassion, and bodhicitta to arise in my mind, I supplicate you.

Then imagine that the guru descends through the aperture of Brahma, and comes to rest in a palace of light concealed in your heart facing upward. This practice of devotion and yearning is guru yoga, and it is imperative to begin every meditation session in this way.

B. Preliminary Instructions

Second, there are the four contemplations: the difficulty of attaining the freedoms and endowments, death and impermanence, the defects of samsara, and the cause and result of karma. If these are new to you, they are explained extensively in the gradual-path texts. It is essential to cultivate conviction in these points so that they arise in your mind. If needed, here is a concise explanation of the fundamental contemplation.

To obtain a basis for the practice of dharma, the freedoms and endowments are perfect. Because sentient beings rarely practice pure virtue, the result is that the freedoms and endowments are difficult to acquire. If one considers other sentient beings such as animals, it is evident that a human life is barely possible. Having now obtained this human life, one must strive in the genuine dharma so that this life is not squandered.

Furthermore, life is unpredictable and the causes of death are numerous, and one cannot be confident that death will not come even today. One must apply the genuine dharma immediately. At the time of death, aside from virtuous and non-virtuous actions, nothing will follow, not food, wealth, possessions, one's home, body, or power. There is no need for these things since they are without even the slightest benefit.

After death, through the power of karma, wherever one is born in the six classes of beings, there is only suffering without even a strand of happiness. Happiness and suffering arise unfailingly as a result of virtuous and non-virtuous deeds. So even at the cost of one's life, one should not engage in negative actions. Practice only virtuous actions and train diligently in this kind of thinking.

At the end of a meditation session, do the seven-branch prayer as many times as possible. In post-meditation put the result of your contemplations into practice. These should be applied in all the preliminary and main practices.

II. The Main Practice: Training in Bodhicitta
According to the second point, there are two parts of the main practice: the attendant meditation on absolute bodhicitta and the principal meditation on relative bodhicitta.

A. Absolute Bodhicitta (Attendant Meditation)
The first part has two sections: in-meditation and post-meditation.
    1. In-meditation
    As for the first section, following the practice of guru yoga, sit with your body straight. Breathing in and out, count your breaths twenty-one times without disturbance to become a suitable vessel for meditation. As for the main practice:

2. Consider all phenomena as a dream.

Apprehended objects, the actual phenomena of the world and its inhabitants, all these appearances are only the confused perception of one's own mind. In fact, they are not truly existent in the least and are therefore like a dream. Thinking in this way, briefly train in this motivation.

Should you wonder if mind itself is real,

3. Examine the nature of unborn awareness.

When looking directly at the essence of one's own mind, there is no color, shape, or form. Nothing whatsoever is established. Since mind has no origin, it is unborn and does not exist from the very beginning. Presently it is not located anywhere, neither inside nor outside the body. Finally, mind is not an object that goes somewhere or ceases to exist. By analyzing and examining mind, you should attain confidence and conviction in the nature of awareness, free from arising, ceasing, and dwelling. Conceptual thoughts about the antidote may arise. You may think, "mind and body are all empty" or "there is neither benefit nor harm in emptiness." If this happens, then

4. The antidote in itself is liberated.

When you look at the nature of the antidote itself with interest in the lack of true existence, then without reference it is liberated naturally. Relax at ease in this nature. These lines present the quintessential instructions that are the ultimate accomplishment of analytical meditation.

5. Rest in the nature of the alaya.

This teaches the actual method of placing the mind. With the seven groups of consciousness free from all activity, there is the essence of all phenomena, the natural state, the alaya. This is indicated by the term "virtuous buddha nature." Rest in the natural state without any thought of the nature existing, without any mental grasping in a state characterized by non-discursive luminous clarity, free from all elaborations. In brief, remain as long as you are able in meditative equilibrium, without following discursive thoughts, in the state of non-conceptual, clear nature of mind. This is placement meditation. Then as before, mix this with the seven-branch prayer.

2. Post-meditation
Contemplation in post-meditation:

6. In post-meditation, be a child of illusion.

In post-meditation, regardless of your activities, remain inseparable from meditative equilibrium. To be like a child of illusion is to continually cultivate the aspiration to realize the lack of true existence. Appearances of self and other, animate and inanimate: all that appears is without true existence.

B. Relative Bodhicitta (Principal Meditation)
The second part, meditation on relative bodhicitta, has three sections: preliminaries, in-meditation, and post-meditation.

1. Preliminaries
To begin, do the preliminary practices as explained above. Then aim to meditate on love and compassion, which is the ground of giving and taking.

Begin by imagining your own mother in front of you. Then think:

> This individual from the beginning of my very existence has protected me with tremendous effort. She is my mother. She alone endured illness, cold, hunger, and so forth. She provided food and clothing, wiped away the filth. And because she taught me what is virtuous and non-virtuous, I am now practicing the dharma. It is because of her immense kindness that

I have met the buddhist teachings. While she herself wanders in the suffering of samsara, experiencing so much pain, she acts on behalf of my own welfare.

Meditate with strong compassion on this.

Once deep compassion has been practiced, not just through words, but has truly blossomed and is established, you must learn to gradually extend it.

All sentient beings from beginningless time have been our mothers just like our present mother. They have all brought us tremendous benefit.

Through reflection, begin by thinking about objects that are easy: friends, relatives, spouses, those suffering intensely in the three lower realms, the poor and wretched. Meditate on those who, though happy in this life, are very evil and will go directly to hell immediately after their death. When one has trained in compassion in this way, then meditate on more troubling objects: enemies, those who have caused you harm, demons and so forth. Finally, meditate on all sentient beings in every direction, thinking:

My own parents experience much suffering unwillingly, which is the cause for future suffering. At this moment, what can be done? To express my gratitude, I should banish what is harmful to them and ensure their comfort and happiness.

Train the mind so the compassion you feel is unbearable.
2. In-meditation
Second,

7. Practice giving and taking alternately.
Mount both upon the breath.

These parents, who are the object of one's compassion, are harmed by suffering directly and indirectly and by the very source of suffering, afflicting emotions.

Think of all the suffering of your mothers and the source of that suffering, all the karma and kleshas. Meditate so that their negativity arises within you. And at the same time, think how happy you would be if you could absorb all their suffering.

Think to yourself:

I send all my own virtue and happiness throughout the three times, my wealth, my bodies to all mother sentient beings, my parents.

Meditate so that each individual receives these delights and cultivate an intense joy as if they can indeed receive them. In order for this to manifest clearly, as you inhale, think that the darkness of all sentient beings' evil deeds, obscurations, and sufferings dissolves into your own heart. Think that all sentient beings have been liberated from their evil deeds and suffering.

As you exhale, imagine your own virtue and joy taking the form of light rays radiating from your nostrils, and being absorbed by all sentient beings. Think that all beings are presently attaining the state of buddhahood. With joy engage this practice of giving and taking with the breath as the actual practice for this session of meditation. Even in the evening try to remember the practice as much as you can. Thus, Shantideva taught this mind training in depth by saying:

Without exchanging my happiness for others' suffering
Buddhahood will not be attained.
Happiness does not exist in samsara.

3. Post-meditation
Third, to apply this in post-meditation practice:

8. Three objects, three poisons, and three roots of virtue.

We ascribe attachment to objects that are appealing or pleasant. Aversion is present when objects are unpleasant or harmful. Stupidity or neutrality are applied with respect to other objects. Recognize these three objects and three poisons when they arise. For example, when attachment arises, think:

> May the attachment of every sentient being be contained by my own attachment. May all sentient beings possess the root of virtue that is free from attachment.

Remind yourself:

> May my attachment take the place of all others' afflictions until they attain buddhahood. May they be liberated from their afflictions.

Anger and so forth can be taken on the path in the same way. Thus, the three poisons become three infinite roots of virtue.

9. In all conduct train with maxims.

At all times, repeat these lines:
From the discourse of the Noble One:

> As their evil ripens in me,
> May my own virtue ripen in them.

From the advice of the Kadampa school:

I offer all gain and victory to precious others, each and every sentient being. I accept all loss and defeat for myself.

From Gyalse Tokme's teachings:

> When every suffering and evil deed of all sentient beings matures in me,
> May all my virtue and happiness bear fruit in them.

10. Begin the sequence of taking with oneself.

To have the ability to take upon oneself the suffering of another, begin the sequence of taking with oneself. Imagine taking on all the suffering that will inevitably ripen for you in the future right now. When that has been cleansed, take on all the suffering of others.

III. Transforming Adversity into the Path of Enlightenment
The third point involves carrying practice into daily life.

11. When the world is full of evil, transform misfortune into the path of awakening.

When suffering permeates one's life due to the fruit of wrongdoing, when glory and wealth are withheld and horrible people cause one harm and so on, it is essential to transform these adverse circumstances that are of immediate concern into the path of awakening. There are three ways of doing this: by relying upon relative bodhicitta, absolute bodhicitta, and special practices.

A. Relative Bodhicitta
For the first way,

12. Realize all faults spring from one source.

No matter what happens to you and your surroundings, big or small, such as sickness in body, mental sufferings, abuse, arguments with enemies, and so on, do not blame outer circumstances by feeling that "so and so, or such and such harmed me." Instead, think in this way:

> These sufferings that befall me result from my own various un-virtuous actions, which are based on my own self-centered motivations from beginningless time until now in samsara. Those desires are all caused by my own mind, which clings to the self where there is no self. I should therefore never blame outside factors, but blame self-centered attachment. I will try to tame this and only this by all means!

Thinking in this way, you should direct the power of all dharmas toward this self-centered attachment.

In *The Way of the Bodhisattva,* Shantideva says:

> In this world, all threats,
> Fears and sufferings spring
> From self-centered attachment,
> So what is the use of protecting this demon?

He also says:

> You have caused me suffering
> For hundreds of lives in samsara.
> Now I remember all those grudges
> And will destroy you, my own contemptible mind.

13. Meditate upon gratitude toward all.

In general, when aiming to attain buddhahood, there is no method of accomplishment that does not rely on sentient beings as objects. Thus for someone who wishes to attain enlightenment, sentient beings and buddhas are equally worthy of deep gratitude and appreciation.

In particular, all sentient beings are worthy of appreciation since there is not one who has not been our father or mother. Moreover, those who bring harm enable us to accumulate merit and purify obscurations. Hence they are friends and allies. Considering their great kindness, practice tonglen. Never get angry even toward dogs or worms. Endeavor to truly benefit even those who cause obstacles.

If you cannot do this, then think and recite:

> May this sentient being or harm-doer swiftly be freed from suffering, attain happiness, and attain the state of buddhahood.

Generate the thought:

> Whatever virtues I cultivate from now on, I shall do so for the welfare of all these beings! This suffering arose because I have inflicted harm upon these beings, whether god or demon, since beginningless time. Now I will offer my own flesh and blood as repayment.

Picture a harmful being before you, and offer your own body while saying:

> May you enjoy whatever you desire, even my own flesh and blood.

With complete renunciation, meditate on this harmful being delighting in your flesh and blood, his mind in undefiled bliss. Arouse the two bodhicittas and contemplate:

> Lacking remedies, I did not even notice the rising of afflicting emotions. Certainly this harmful being, by summoning these

negativities, is a teacher or buddha. By motivating me to train in bodhicitta, I feel tremendous appreciation for this being.

Also, if sickness or suffering arises, reflect wholeheartedly:

If this had not occurred, I would be distracted by the concerns of this life and never turn my mind toward dharma. Because of this illness, I am reminded and resolved to follow dharma. So it is the enlightened activity of the guru or the precious jewels. I am incredibly grateful.

In brief, a worldly being is someone whose attitude and conduct seek to secure benefit for oneself. A dharmic being is someone whose attitude and conduct seek to secure the benefit of others. Langri Tangpa says:

I reveal for you as profound a teaching as there exists. Look and understand! All faults belong to oneself. All positive qualities belong to precious sentient beings. This is the essential point: offer gain and victory to others, take loss and defeat for oneself. There is no other meaning than this.

B. Absolute Bodhicitta
For the second way,

14. Meditate upon illusory appearance as the four kayas.
This is the unsurpassable protection of emptiness.

In general, all appearance, or in particular, bad conditions, are like dreams where one is burnt in fire or drowned in water. Our mind grasps at illusory appearance as something substantial. Now clearly recognize that there is nothing substantial in appearance, not even a bit. Just stay in the state without any attachment to mere appearance. When you do so, the emptiness nature is the dharmakaya, the clear appearance is the nirmanakaya, the union of the two is the sambhogakaya, and the union of the three is the svabhavikakaya. Rest in meditative equilibrium, where there is no substantial arising, dwelling, or ceasing. This is the pith instruction for recognizing the four kayas. It is the armor of the view. This protection boundary of emptiness is an unsurpassable pith instruction to vanquish illusory appearances.

C. Special Practices
As for the third way,

15. The four practices are the best of means.

The four practices are:
    i. accumulating merit
    ii. confessing wrongdoings
    iii. offering tormas to gods and demons
    iv. offering tormas to dakinis and dharma protectors
These are the best of means to turn difficult circumstances into the path.

    i. Accumulating merit
Although we desire happiness, there are times when only suffering comes. In those times, think in this way:

> What I need to do is to abandon wrongdoings, the cause of suffering. This happened because of my lacking an accumulation of the causes of happiness. I should therefore accumulate more merit.

For example, make offerings to your guru and the Three Jewels, venerate and make offerings to monastic communities, offer tormas to demons, offer butter lamps, make tsatsas, circumambulate, and do prostrations. In this way, with all three doors accumulate merit as much as you can. In addition, take refuge, arouse bodhicitta, and in particular, sincerely practice the seven-branch prayer and make mandala offerings.

> If it is good for me to be sick, bless me to be sick.
> If it is good for me to heal, bless me to heal.
> If it is good for me to die, bless me to die.

Make supplications in this way to cease all your hopes and fears.

ii. Confessing wrongdoings
Have the same aspiration as above and regret your past wrongdoings. This is the power of complete remorse. Also think in this way:

> I shall never repeat these reprehensible deeds from now on!

This is the power of turning away from faults. Then take refuge and arouse bodhicitta. This is the power of support. Make efforts in the sixfold remedies, such as meditating on emptiness, reciting dharani and mantra, making the previously mentioned supplications, and the rest in order to eradicate all hopes and fears. To act in this way is the power of application. Practice these four powers until you are proficient.

iii. Offering tormas to gods and demons
Think in this way:

> You chased after me as a response to my previous karmic debt and revealed these debts to me. I really appreciate it. Now destroy me completely. Make all sentient beings' sufferings, unwanted sickness, and all fears ripen upon my body. Make all sentient beings free from suffering!

Supplicate like this and lead harmful beings to activities of dharma.

If this is difficult for you, make a torma, practice love and kindness, and do tonglen. Then pray like this:

> I will help you in whatever way from now on, so please don't create any obstacles to my dharma practice.

iv. Offering tormas to dakinis and dharma protectors

Pray that all circumstances adverse to accomplishing the dharma are tamed, and that all activities for accomplishing good circumstances are brought to you. In particular, pray that all hopes and fears cease with the prayer mentioned above. The next verse explains the method for using unexpected circumstances as the path.

16. Use whatever you face as a practice immediately.

When you suddenly encounter sickness, obstructing spirits, or negative emotions, or when you see others are harmed by unfavorable circumstances, remind yourself to practice tonglen. If you have any virtuous thoughts or engage in positive actions, wish that all sentient beings naturally engage in dharmic activities far superior to yours. Do the practice in the same way too when any happiness or joy arises.

And if you have any bad thoughts or engage in negative actions without control, wish that all sentient beings' bad thoughts or wrongdoings are gathered into your thoughts or actions.

In brief, whatever you do, eating, sleeping, or walking around, think about others' benefit. Whatever conditions you encounter, good or bad, immediately apply mind training.

IV. An Explanation of the Practices as a Way of Life

The fourth point teaches a summary of practice for one's whole life in two parts: what to do during this life, and what to do at the moment of death.

A. What to Do during This Life
The first part:

17. The pith instructions briefly summarized:
apply the five strengths.

The five strengths summarize the key points of practice as a unity of many essential instructions for practicing the holy dharma. First is the strength of motivation. In order to generate strong motivation in the mind, think the following:

> From this time onward until enlightenment, or at least until I die, and particularly this year and this month, and especially from today until tomorrow, I must never be separated from the two aspects of bodhicitta.

Second is the strength of familiarization. Whatever activities you are engaged in, whether virtuous, harmful, or neutral, sustain your mindfulness and awareness, and train again and again in the two aspects of bodhicitta. In short, train in bodhicitta as your main practice of virtue.

Third is the strength of virtuous seeds. In order to give rise to and further increase bodhicitta, never be self-satisfied with your efforts. Always apply yourself fully to virtuous deeds of body, speech, and mind.

Fourth is the strength of remorse. Whenever thoughts of self-importance arise, think:

> Previously, from time without beginning, you have made me experience different kinds of suffering while spinning in samsara.

In this life as well, every bit of wrongdoing and suffering that arises has only come from you. There is no happiness when associating with you. So from now on I will do whatever I can to destroy and subdue you.

By thinking like this, utterly cast off thoughts of ego-cherishing.

Fifth is the strength of aspiration. At the end of any virtuous activity, think:

May I alone guide all sentient beings to the level of buddhahood. Especially from this very moment until enlightenment, may I never forget the two aspects of precious bodhicitta, and may they grow continually ever stronger, even while dreaming. Whatever adverse circumstances might arise, may they become a force to aid in bodhicitta practice.

Set your mind like this at its core and dedicate all virtue to this purpose.

B. What to Do at the Moment of Death

The second part: what are the instructions from this tradition for the moment of death?

18. The Mahayana instructions for the transference of consciousness are the five strengths. Conduct is vital.

When a person who has trained in this teaching is stricken with illness and approaching certain death, they should practice the five strengths. First, the strength of virtuous seeds is to give away all one's possessions without a trace of attachment, expectation, or clinging. Generally speaking, they can be given to the guru and the jewels, and in particular, they can be given wherever they will bring the most benefit.

The strength of aspiration is to pray with a one-pointed mind and perform the seven-branch offering prayer. If one cannot, then pray:

> Whatever roots of virtue I have accumulated throughout the three times and in all my future lives to come, may I never forget, but train in and increase precious bodhicitta. May I meet an authentic guru who reveals this teaching. May I accomplish these aspirations through the blessings of the guru and the jewels.

The strength of remorse is to think:

> This self-importance has led me to suffer countless births. And in this life, I must also endure the suffering of death. Ultimately there is nothing that dies, as self and mind have no existence. By all means I must bring down this self-importance that thinks in terms of "I am sick, I am dying."

The strength of motivation is to think:

> At the time of death, in the intermediate state and in all my future rebirths, I must never be separated from the two kinds of bodhicitta.

The strength of familiarization is to bring to mind the two kinds of bodhicitta practiced previously. The main point is to practice these strengths one-pointedly, but the accompanying actions are also important. Physically, you should sit in the seven-point posture. But if that is not possible, lie down on your right side with the right hand under your cheek, and block the right nostril with the little finger. While breathing through the left nostril, begin meditating on love and compassion. Join the practice of sending and taking with the coming and going of the breath. Then, without grasping to anything, rest evenly in the wisdom that knows samsara and nirvana, birth and death, and so forth, are all appearances of the mind, and that mind itself cannot be defined as concrete. Within this state, continue to breathe as well as you can. It is said that there are many great instructions for the time of death, but none more wonderful than this.

A pith instruction for the transference of consciousness that employs a salve states:

Apply to the top of your head a substance consisting of the ash of burned, unspoiled seashells and a magnet mixed with wild honey.

V. Measures of Proficiency in Mind Training
The fifth point teaches the measures of proficiency in mind training.

19. All dharma agrees at a single point.

Since the entire aim of all dharma, both in the Mahayana and Hinayana, is to tame ego-clinging, as you practice dharma or endeavor in mind training, self-importance should decrease. If your efforts in dharma practice do not reduce self-importance, such practice is meaningless. Since this is the standard of a dharma practitioner, it is said to be the scale that weighs the progress of the practitioner.

20. Of the two witnesses, rely on the main one.

Another's measure of your dharma practice may be one testimony, but ordinary people don't know what is hidden in your mind and may be pleased by only a few improvements in your conduct. Never being embarrassed by your state of mind is one sign of proficiency in mind training. So do not be attached to others' testimonies, but rely principally on the testimony of your own mind.

21. Always maintain a joyful attitude.

When there is never any fear or despair no matter what misfortune and suffering arise, when such circumstances are taken as an aid to mind training, and you always have the help of a joyful mind, these are signs that you have acquired proficiency in mind training. When adverse circumstances arise, meditate joyfully. Furthermore, train to take on with joy all the misfortunes of others.

22. You have reached proficiency if you can practice even while distracted.

As an example, a skilled horseman does not fall from his horse even while distracted. Likewise, if you are able to take adverse circumstances that suddenly arise as aids to mind training even without intending to do so, then you are well trained. Enemies, friends, troublemakers, happiness, and suffering, in the very moment any of these arise, the two bodhicittas arise effortlessly and distinctly.

These four slogans are signs of your training in bodhicitta. They are not signs that you need not train further. Until buddhahood is attained, you must train to strengthen your bodhicitta.

VI. Commitments of Mind Training
The sixth point concerns the vows of mind training.

23. Always train in the three basic principles.

There are three general principles:

Do not contradict the oaths undertaken in mind training. Remain unsullied by the taint of transgressions in whatever vows you have made, including the subtle points of individual liberation, bodhicitta, and Vajrayana training.

Do not become lost in inconsiderate actions or hope that others notice you have no self-cherishing. Give up improper behavior such as destroying shrines, cutting down sacred trees, disturbing sacred water, and putting on a show, seemingly without care of self, by associating with lepers, vagabonds, and so forth. Act with pure stainless character.

Do not fall into biased opinions. You may be patient with people harming you but be unable to bear the injuries of gods or demons, or the other way around. You may be patient with friends but be unable to tolerate enemies. You may endure these but not be able to bear suffering and other pain. You may even be able to endure all that but let dharma slip when you are comfortable. The commitment of mind training is to abandon biased opinions. Always train in this.

24. Transform your attitude and remain natural.

While changing and reversing your previous self-cherishing and lack of concern for others, take on the welfare of others as a crucial task. Realize that all mind training must be carried out through minor deeds that have major effects. Remain natural and silent. Like all others who are in accord with dharma, behave outwardly as a friend. Mature your mind stream without the notice of others.

25. Do not speak about the downfalls of others.

Do not utter unpleasant words about others' worldly flaws such as being blind or stupid, or spiritual faults such as forsaken vows and so forth. Speak with acceptable, pleasing words combined with a calm, relaxed smile.

26. Do not ponder others' business.

In general, do not ponder others' business. In particular, do not ponder the faults of those who follow the practice of dharma. Think instead:

> Perceiving their faults is due to my own impure perception. This person is not really like that. Thinking otherwise is similar to those who saw faults in the Buddha.

Put an end to your own faulty attitude.

27. Train with the strongest emotions first.

Examine whichever affliction is strongest within you. In the beginning concentrate all dharma practice on subduing that affliction.

28. Abandon any expectation of fruition.

To cultivate mind training in the hope of subjugating gods and demons, in the hope of being perceived as "good" or labeled as "helpful" by accepting blame—these are all pretensions to be abandoned. In a word, abandon any such hope of a self-centered result, such as wishing to obtain ease, enjoyment, and reputation in this life, the happiness of gods and men, or perfect peace for oneself in future lives.

29. Abstain from toxic food.

Abstain from any good endeavor motivated by clinging to things as real or by self-importance as you would toxic food. Train in non-grasping at dream-like appearance.

30. Do not be a loyalist.

Be free of loyalty to your mundane concerns. For instance, no matter where you are or how much time has passed, you cannot forget those who have harmed you. Let go of the irreversible grudge brought on by injury done to you in malice. Retaliate instead with beneficial thoughts and deeds.

31. Do not be contentious.

Generally speaking, you should not take pleasure in exposing another's flaws. In particular, do not speak maliciously of another in response to insults they have issued you. Moreover, even if blamed, reply with silence, and strive always to extol the virtue of others.

32. Do not wait in ambush.

Mentally fixating on another's offensive act and refusing to forget about it although many years have passed, one finally enacts revenge in a moment of ambush. Abandon that attack by avenging harm with help. Do not fixate on the turmoil of inner negativity as harmful. Cultivate love and compassion alone.

33. Do not pounce upon vulnerability.

Do not make remarks that produce discomfort in the minds of others by delving into their concealed flaws, by insinuating at vulnerabilities, by draining out the vital life force of non-humans with mantras and so forth.

34. Do not transfer the dzo's load onto the ox.

To unload upon others the unfortunate responsibilities that have befallen you, or to consign hardship that has come upon you to others through deceit is like transferring the load of a dzo onto an ox. Refrain from doing so.

35. Do not be competitive.

During a horse race, the aim is to be the fastest. Similarly, among equal practitioners there is the hope of gaining honor and renown in order to become superior. Thinking up various means by which to acquire worldly wealth as well as striving toward it must be abandoned. Whether or not to become famous and receive gain and honor should be of no concern.

36. Do not twist the practice.

If you accept loss and defeat in the present time with the desire to benefit from it in the long run, or if you practice mind training with the hope of pacifying sickness or malicious spirits, or to reverse negative circumstances, these are like chanting a fabricated ransom ritual. Your practice is wrong. Do not do this. Instead, whatever happiness or sorrow arises, meditate without hope, fear, arrogance, or doubt.

Gyalse Tokme says:

> Mind training that is done in such a manner is like a vulture. It is a skillful means to benefit malevolent spirits. If you practice in that way, it is no different from practicing Bön.

He taught that dharma activity must be an effective antidote against disturbing emotions and discursive thoughts.

Starting with this example, consider what is known as mistaken dharma practice: wrong view is an eternalist or nihilist view. Wrong meditation is clinging to any sublime state. Wrong conduct is anything that is in disagreement with the three vows. Wrong dharma is anything contrary to the view and conduct of what has been authentically taught as the holy dharma, whether it comes from you or someone else, from someone superior or inferior. It is also said that mistaken dharma will hurl you into samsara and lower rebirths. For example, it is like applying the wrong remedy or ingesting the wrong medicine for an illness.

There are some people who profess a composed work or a terma of an individual as mistaken dharma without having analyzed the words or meaning in a single chapter to see whether or not the composed dharma or terma teaching is authentic. It appears as though their proclamations are based on attachments to their own position and tenet system, or based on personal circumstances like envy and so forth.

It has been said that no one but a buddha is able to conceive the aptitude of an individual's mind stream. So even though you may not like an individual who is supposed to possess an authentic view and conduct, it does not mean that what he has accomplished is mistaken dharma. For example, a merchant can sell gold of excellent quality or something of little value, but it does not make him a better or worse merchant. Therefore, the Buddha said again and again:

Rely not upon individuals. Rely upon the dharma. The understanding of what is evidently a point of great importance is why I have made this additional statement.

37. Do not bring a god down to the level of a demon.

This means that if you cultivate mind training and your own mind becomes rigid with pride and conceit, it is as though you have brought a god down to the level of a demon, and the dharma has become non-dharma. The more you meditate on dharma or mind training, the more your own mind should be moving toward becoming tamed. You should act like the lowest servant to everyone.

38. Do not seek out others' suffering as the limbs of your delight.

Do not think: "If my patron were to fall ill and die, I would receive food and resources," or "If this fellow monk or these dharma friends were to die, I would receive their books and holy objects," or "If my colleague were to die, I alone would get the merit," or "Wouldn't it be wonderful if my enemy were to die?"

In brief, you should not wish the suffering of others to become the limbs of your own happiness. Such hopes must be forsaken.

VII. Guidelines for Mind Training

The seventh point provides guidelines for mind training.

39. Use one practice for everything.

As it is said, whether eating, dressing, sleeping, traveling, or sitting, utilize one practice. Always have the intention to benefit others.

40. Use a single corrective for everything.

Analysis itself is used as a corrective for analysis. If, while meditating on mind training, adverse circumstances arise, whether you are pierced by slander and belittled or harmed by demons, if quarreling with enemies and disturbing emotions increase, or if you have no desire in your heart to meditate, remind yourself:

> In the whole universe there are many sentient beings who have problems like mine.

Then arouse compassion for them all by thinking:

> In addition to these unwanted situations, may all the unwanted sufferings of sentient beings be gathered here.

Use the single corrective of exchanging yourself for others.

41. Two things to do: one at the beginning, one at the end.

As soon as you rise in the morning, generate a strong thought:

Today, I will be inseparable from the two bodhicittas.

During the daytime make sure to retain them continuously with mindfulness. Then at night when you lie down to sleep, examine the thoughts and actions of your day. If they are contrary to bodhicitta, quantify and acknowledge them, confess them, and vow that henceforth such actions will not arise. If there has been no obstruction, meditate joyfully and aspire that in the future, you and other beings will be able to engage in bodhicitta, the most supreme method. Always train in these two activities. For infractions of vows and so forth, one should also contemplate in the same way.

42. Whichever of the two arises, be patient.

If one becomes utterly destitute with great suffering, reflect upon previous karma. Refrain from being resentful or depressed and strive to purify obstacles and negativities by seeking to take up all the wrongdoings and misery of others. If one has great happiness and comfort, has attained perfect wealth and servants, do not give sway to indifference and carelessness. Utilize that wealth to favor virtue and to transform one's power for the good of others. Pray that all beings are endowed with such comfort and joy. In short, whichever of the two arises, joy or sorrow, be patient.

43. Protect the two as dearly as your life.

Because all present and future happiness comes from observing the two sets of precepts, take care, even if your life is at risk, to protect the general precepts of dharma, which include the three vows along with the particular precepts and commitments of mind training. Furthermore, whatever you do, do not fetter your actions with thoughts only for yourself. Observe the two precepts with consideration for the welfare of others.

44. Train in the three difficulties.

The first difficulty is to recognize the afflicting emotions. The middle difficulty is to subdue them. The final difficulty is to break their continuity. First, as soon as they arise, recognize that they are afflicting emotions. Then, having increased the strength of their remedies, abandon them. Finally, set a resolved intention that they will never arise again. In these three you must train.

45. Take up the three principal causes.

The principal causes of accomplishing the dharma are: an appropriate guru, a workable mind to apply the practice through the appropriate methods of dharma, and the conducive conditions for dharmic accomplishment (food, clothing, etc.). If you have gathered these three, cultivate joy and pray for the completion of these three in others. If they are not complete, cultivate compassion toward others. Take upon yourself the deficiencies of all sentient beings, namely the lack of these three principal causes. Pray that you and all others may possess these three.

46. Practice to not let the three degenerate.

Because all qualities of Mahayana dharma depend upon the guru, do not let faith and devotion toward the guru degenerate. Because mind training is the quintessence of the Mahayana dharma, do not let enthusiasm toward meditation on mind training degenerate. Also, do not allow discipline in the three vows to degenerate. Train in these three aspects.

47. Remain inseparable from the three.

The three faculties of body, speech, and mind should always remain inseparable from the roots of virtue and be devoid of misdeeds.

48. Practice impartially toward everything. Deep and comprehensive mastery overall is essential.

Without partiality for certain things, mind training alone should pervade all that might arise as the object of mind, the good and the bad, sentient beings, the four elements, non-sentient beings, non-human beings, and so forth. In this regard, achieving mastery from the depth of your heart is essential so that your practice is not merely mouthed words.

49. Always meditate on whatever is most challenging.

Meditate by skillfully cultivating extraordinary love and compassion toward: those who by the influence of their deeds are mentally disagreeable, objects that are difficult to engage by mind training (such as hostile enemies or troublesome, obstructing forces), those who in response to help are ungrateful and bring harm, competitors or rivals, as well as useless associates who are naturally harmful. In particular, eliminate any cause of trouble to important relationships like those with your teacher and parents.

50. Do not rely on other factors.

Do not depend on any positive or negative conditions, good or bad health, abundance or scarcity, kind or unkind criticism, troubles or freedom from troubles. If favorable conditions are assembled, utilize the good conditions and train the mind. If those conditions do not assemble, utilize the lack of good conditions and cultivate the two bodhicittas. In short, independent of your own situation or external factors, always remain inseparable from the practitioner's mind training.

51. Practice what is essential now.

From beginningless time you have taken up innumerable forms, all of which have been without the slightest significance. In the future, a gathering of conducive conditions similar to the present conditions will not arise. Now on this occasion, having obtained a human form and having met the true dharma, you must practice the essential points to accomplish the lasting goal for lifetimes to come. In this regard, goals for the future are more important than goals for this life. In the future, liberation is more important than samsara. The benefit of others is more important than the benefit of self. Of the two, teachings and practice, practice is more important. And the practice of bodhicitta is more important than other practices. Moreover, fervent meditation on your guru's oral instruction is more important than the analytical meditation of scriptural logic. To train while abiding on your cushion is more important than any other path of activity.

52. Do not dwell in misunderstanding.

Abandon the six misunderstandings. To patiently endure the hardships of subduing enemies, caring for friends, working for material profit, and the like while not tolerating the difficulties of accomplishing dharma is mistaken patience. To have aspirations of glory, wealth, and happiness in this life while having no interest in thoroughly practicing pure dharma is mistaken aspiration. To relish the wealth of material possessions while having no taste for the three wisdoms is mistaken taste. To not generate compassion toward those who engage in wrongdoing while cultivating compassion toward those undergoing hardship on account of the dharma is mistaken compassion. To engage men who look to you in the glorification of this life while not connecting them with the dharma is mistaken care. To cultivate joy in the suffering of enemies and the unhappiness of others while having no joy in the virtue and happiness of nirvana or samsara is mistaken joy. All of these six should be completely abandoned.

53. Do not be sporadic.

Those who sometimes practice and sometimes do not practice will not develop a definitive knowledge of dharma. Therefore, do not have many different focal points; practice mind training single-pointedly.

54. Train wholeheartedly.

Without involvement in distraction, exert yourself exclusively in mind training, casting aside everything to practice in this one direction.

55. Find liberation through both reflection and analysis.

One must attain liberation from afflictions and from ego-clinging through constant reflection and analysis of one's own mind stream. Contemplate objects that give rise to afflictions. Vigorously examine whether or not they arise. If they do arise, earnestly make use of their antidote. Look at self-cherishing to see what it truly is. If it does not exist as such, examine it with respect to an object of attachment or aversion. At that time, if self-cherishing is born, immediately discard it through the remedy of exchanging self and other.

56. Do not feel the world owes you.

Refrain from boasting about your own kindness toward others, since the point of this is in fact to make others more important than yourself. Since all the time and hardship in becoming skilled, respectable, and practicing the dharma has been for your own benefit, it would be absurd to boast to others. Do not trade boasts with others. According to the instructions of Drom Tonpa, it is said, "Do not expect much of people. Pray to the yidam."

57. Do not be reactive.

Refrain from thoughts of jealousy toward others. If others harm or belittle you in public, do not respond. Do not let your mind stream become agitated. As Potowa said:

As dharma practitioners, we have not made dharma an antidote to self-grasping. So our tolerance is more thin-skinned than a blister. We are more reactive than Tsang-tsen. Therefore this is ineffective dharma. To be effective, dharma must remedy self-grasping.

58. Do not be temperamental.

Do not devour the minds of your companions by expressing every slight mood of momentary happiness or unhappiness.

59. Do not self-aggrandize.

Do not seek to receive another's expression of gratitude and words of thanks in return for your own practice of dharma, help to others, virtuous actions, and the like. In short, reject seeking to create fame or reputation. Similarly, all of these instructions are means to prevent degeneration and to develop mind training. In summary, Gyalse Rinpoche said:

Throughout your life, train properly by means of both kinds of bodhicitta in both meditation and post-meditation. You must attain the confidence of this training.

Strive to follow these instructions.

Concluding Verses

Degeneration Turning into the Path of Bodhi: Pith Instructions from Serlingpa

Transforming the rampant five degenerations
Into the path of enlightenment,
These pith instructions, ambrosia's essence,
Are a direct transmission from Serlingpa.

The five degenerations of time period, sentient beings, lifespan, afflictions, and views proliferate, while joyful, harmonious conditions are few. Antidotes from other teachings are not effective because of widespread discordant and contrary conditions. Those adept in mind training will progress in their virtuous practice however great the adversity, just as a fire will grow and grow as more wood is added. With a distinctive feature that others lack, this teaching alone transforms all affliction and adversity into the path of enlightenment. The essence of ambrosia, these pith instructions will enrich one's being and benefit everyone of high or low capacity. These teachings are a direct transmission from the great Lord Serlingpa, the very kindest of Lord Atisha's three gurus.

Through awakening the karmic residue of previous training,
My own conviction was deeply stirred.
Thereby, I utterly dismissed suffering and criticism,
And requested advice to tame self-clinging.
So now, when I die, there are no regrets.

Awakened to previous karmic residue, the great spiritual friend, Chekawa himself, through great difficulties and fervent longing for this teaching alone, attained the root of all dharma, the instruction to tame ego-clinging, from Atisha's Kagyu lineage of master and student. Having trained well, his exalted mind revered others more than himself. The entanglements of selfish desires never befell him again. With the discovery of inner confidence through ultimate realization, the essential meaning of crossing the threshold of dharma, he regretted nothing.

The contents of the last two verses were spoken by the author in conclusion.

Supplementary Instructions of the Transmission Lineage

This profound teaching on mind training is itself a comfort to sorrow if you are by yourself. Not only that, mind training in itself is enough to bring all happiness and suffering onto the path. When the profound dharma enflames negative karma, the mind is likewise enflamed. If we are active, we want to sit. If we sit, we want to go. In such a case, meditate in this way:

If your disposition is like this,
Such a resting place is best,
Such a frame of mind is just fine.
And through your resilience,
Hooray! You won't be born in hell.
Hooray! You won't be boiled or baked.

Fearing lower realms,
I should be driven further to self-reproach.
I should be able to endure hardship and meager food,
Accept paltry garments and lowly portions,
Scorn joy and pain, and cultivate antidotes.

In accordance with what has been taught in *The Stages of the Awakened Warrior,* a critical dialogue with oneself strikes the crucial point.

When sick, illness is the nurse. With respect to the medicine, nurse, companions, and so forth, when you falsely charge them believing that they could do better than this and become resentful, in your mind think:

For this sickness, no other is at fault. Self-grasping is solely to blame.

You have tried all these treatments in the past and they still have not worked to free you from this suffering. Stop thinking another medicine or nurse can help you. From now on, remind yourself:

Ego-clinging, be satisfied you are getting what you want.

In addition to that, train in taking the illness and negative forces of others upon yourself.

As the noble Serlingpa taught:

Vanquish all burgeoning thoughts.
Every antidote is a conquering strike.
Condense all goals into one.
Resolve all paths into one.
These are the four remedies, the properties of complete
    purification.
They are needed to tame the wild.
To deal with mistaken enterprise and unwholesome allegiances,
In this dark age, they are vital.

Quell the swelling of discursive thoughts as soon as they arise by dwelling in emptiness. This comprises mind training. From the outset, all antidotes are not just gradual habituations. As soon as afflicting emotions arise, crush, trample, smash, and destroy them. Make no preparations for pursuing a variety of different ambitions either currently or ultimately. Focus solely on whatever benefits the mind and obliterate ego-clinging as much as possible. Since freedom from ego-grasping constitutes awakening, this approach serves. Hence there is no need to evaluate the gradients of the path. These four teachings encapsulate every remedy with respect to complete purification.

Adverse circumstances are spiritual friends.
Demonic influences are emanations of the victorious ones.
Sickness is the broom for misdeeds and obscurations.
Suffering is the ever-shifting display of the ultimate nature.
These four teachings thoroughly address afflicting emotions.
They are needed to tame the wild.
To deal with mistaken enterprise and unwholesome allegiances,
In this dark age, they are vital.

Out of misfortune, you can accumulate merit, work with obscurations, possess mindfulness of the sublime dharma, benefit from understanding, and so forth. Thus misfortune fulfills the role of a spiritual friend.

Evading adverse circumstances is unnecessary. The sorcery of gods and demonic spirits and the harm inflicted by malicious forces are helpful in magnifying virtue and spiritual practice. As such, they are the emanations of the teacher and buddhas and thus there is no need to fear them. Engaging properly in the sublime dharma incites former karma and misfortune, causing various physical illnesses to ensue continually. And when this befalls you, even mere small headaches, not to mention severe maladies, are purifying, sweeping and driving away all wrongdoings accumulated since beginningless time. The sutras say again and again, cultivate joy in sickness. When the experience of suffering comes, by looking into the true essence of pain, it dawns as emptiness. However intense the suffering, since it is the ever-shifting display of the ultimate nature, there is no need to be disheartened. If all this befalls you, it is excellent because it allows you to take them as support in practice. Understand the instruction to implement, not avoid, the four teachings on dealing with deeply disturbing emotions.

> The harness of happiness is great.
> The resolution of suffering is great.
> The utterly undesired is the primordial wish.
> Bad omens are accepted as sacred.
> These four teachings are the antidotes of other countermeasures.
> They are needed to tame the wild.
> To deal with mistaken enterprise and unwholesome allegiances,
> In this dark age, they are vital.

When at ease and happy in body and mind, the wish to do a multiplicity of things unrelated to the dharma arises. With respect to the actual essence of feeling happiness, observe its insubstantiality. Bring this mere appearance of happiness onto the path by offering it to all sentient beings. To not be absorbed by this appearance of happiness by remaining capably steady—this is the harness of happiness. When suffering comes, do not despair but rather see its true essence as emptiness and it will dissolve. In addition to these appearances of suffering, take on the unwanted misery of all sentient beings. Ability and stability in this are the resolution of perpetual suffering. When you encounter anything unwanted or unwished for, those things are actually your original wish and intention by being the support for demolishing self-cherishing. In your mind remain bolstered and at ease with the thought:

Ego-clinging, this is what you wanted. Let this utterly crush you.

When ominous signs or apparitions arise, how do you take them? A constellation of thoughts ensues, with the question of what is the best thing to do. When this happens, think:

This must be happening for a reason. How excellent this is happening. Stack all inauspicious omens upon this self-cherishing!

And rest without pride or doubt. These four teachings are countermeasures for the impotence of other antidotes.

Ego is the root of flaws.
This is a teaching to renounce it completely.
Others are the wellspring of positive qualities.
This is a teaching to accept them totally.
These two teachings encapsulate the antidotes.
They are needed to tame the wild.
To deal with mistaken enterprise and unwholesome allegiances,
In this dark age, they are vital.

In brief, the entire fundamental basis of mind training can be consolidated into these two directives: to completely abandon self-interest and to wholly embrace the welfare of others. Thereby, they comprise the ultimate meaning of these instructions. Hold them as the root of practice.

Overturn whatever mistakes and look directly at what is.
Relax freely and rest at ease.
Accept that unbound, they will be liberated.

If your mind wanders outward, chasing after however many or whatever minor afflicting emotions and discursive thoughts may arise, you are not any different from an ordinary person, which means you are on the wrong path. Turn the mind further inward and observe its true, naked essence. Observing thus, there is nothing to be seen. In that moment, relax and let go into that emptiness. Residing in this relaxed ease, however many numerous thoughts or emotions arise, if you are not tied to them, they will be naturally liberated and become the accumulation of wisdom. This is the heart of the meditation stage of absolute bodhicitta.

As stated above, the oral instruction lineage of mind training is based on divine Lord Atisha's tradition, which gathers all essential meanings of the practices from each individual tradition into seven points. Among the large number of commentaries on the teaching, detailed or concise, the content of this text is carefully compiled based on the commentaries by the great noble one, Gyalse Rinpoche Tokme, and venerable Kunga Nyingpo. It is therefore the ambrosia essence of the speech of great past masters. This text was compiled primarily for beginners to understand easily and solely out of my earnest intention to benefit them.

The root of the sutra and mantra path,
The quintessence of all sacred dharma,
So profound but easy to practice,
Marvelous, arises from all teachings.
It is difficult to hear such profound dharma.
Upon hearing, it is difficult to apply.
Those who possess the treasure of merit to practice this
Are more rare these days than gold upon earth.

So many words are thus cause for weariness.
Nevertheless by means of the supreme intention to benefit others,
And through the virtue of writing this,
May all living beings perfect the two bodhicittas.

This text was written by Lodro Thaye, a servant of the kind protectors Karmapa and Situ, in the retreat land of All Goodness and Great Bliss Luminosity at Palpung monastery. It was composed at the persistent request of Karma Thutob, who is well learned in the five sciences, and at the recent urging of the supreme nirmanakaya Karma Thabkhe Namrol, who assumes an unassailable commitment and oath to precious bodhicitta, as well as in response to the insistent appeal of Lama Karma Ngedon and others fortunate in their dedication to accomplishment who seek to elucidate their spiritual practice. May this work benefit all beings.

May virtue and goodness flourish!

Lojong Lineage Supplication:
Relieving the Pain from Devotion

To the Buddha, Lord of Sages, the regent Maitreya, the loving one,
Venerable Asanga, the supreme scholar Vasubandhu,
Two main disciples of Svatantrika, Gunamitra,
And Haribhadra, at your feet I supplicate.
Grant your blessings so that I can perfect the bodhicitta of love
    and compassion,
And the ability to dismiss and dispel.

To Gang-pel, the Elder and Younger Kusalis,
Dharmakirti, the protector Atisha,
Dromtonpa, Potowa, Sharawa,

And yogi Chekawa, I supplicate.
Grant your blessings so that I can perfect the bodhicitta of love
and compassion,
And the ability to dismiss and dispel.

To Chilbupa, Osel Lama,
Lhading, Changchup Bumpa, Kun Gyaltsen,
Yonten Palwa, great scholar Dewa-pal,
Zhonnu, renowned for four teachings, I supplicate.
Grant your blessings so that I can perfect the bodhicitta of love
and compassion,
And the ability to dismiss and dispel.

To the bodhisattva Sonam Drakpa, and glorious Tokme Zangpo,
Yonten Lodro, Zhonnu Lodro,
Great pandita Shakya Chokden, Kunga Chokdrup,
Jetsun Drolchok, at your feet I supplicate.
Grant your blessings so that I can perfect the bodhicitta of love
and compassion,
And the ability to dismiss and dispel.

To Lungrig Gyamtso, Omniscient Taranatha,
The two regents, Yonten Gon,
Gonpo Paljol, Gonpo Dakpa,
Gonpo Namgyal, I supplicate.
Grant your blessings so that I can perfect the bodhicitta of love
and compassion,
And the ability to dismiss and dispel.

To the feet of Tsewang Norbu, Thinle Shinta,
Tenpa Nyinje, the accomplished Lodro,
Karma Lhaktong, Zhenphen Ozer,

And all the root masters, I supplicate.
Grant your blessings so that I can perfect the bodhicitta of love
and compassion,
And the ability to dismiss and dispel.

Grant your blessings so that I can establish the foundation of revulsion and renunciation. May the two kinds of perfect and supreme bodhicitta, secret of reversing karma according to the Mahayana, be born, remain firm, and progress further.

Grant your blessings so that I can reverse the ground of the eight worldly dharmas, cut ego-clinging at its very root, and fully cultivate altruism. May I perfect mind training, which has the power to take all appearance as a support for the path of enlightenment.

Having realized the absolute truth, emptiness free from arising, dwelling, and ceasing, and the relative truth, illusory mode of interdependent origination, for as long as samsara exists and for the benefit of all beings as limitless as space, may I spontaneously attain the level of omniscience.

This prayer was composed by Lodro Thaye as another branch of lojong instructions. May it be auspicious!

The Aspiration Prayer of Mind Training: Entering the Ocean-Like Mind of Bodhicitta

Supreme Lord Avalokiteshvara
And all buddhas and bodhisattvas,
Through your sincere and authentic kindness,
For myself and others and all beings as vast as space,
May supreme bodhicitta arise.

When sentient beings engaged in aggression
Experience the hot and cold hells,
May the cause and effect of their suffering be absorbed into me.
My mind of loving kindness
And all the roots of virtue from non-aggression
I give to beings whose numbers are equal to space.
By emptying the angry hell realms,
May they obtain the sublime mirror-like wisdom
Of the Vajra family of Avalokiteshvara.

When engaged in greed and desire,
Experiencing the hunger and thirst of hungry ghosts,
May the cause and effect of their suffering be absorbed into me.
My mind of renunciation
And all the virtuous roots of non-attachment
I give to all beings who are equal to space.
By emptying the realm of stingy hungry ghosts,
May they attain the supreme wisdom of discriminating awareness,
The Lotus family of Avalokiteshvara.

Those engaged in ignorance,
Like a dull and foolish animal,
May the cause and effect of such suffering be absorbed into me.
My wisdom, learned and innate,

And all virtuous roots of non-ignorance
I give to beings who are equal to space.
By emptying the realm of ignorant animals,
May they obtain the wisdom of dharmadhatu,
The Buddha family of Avalokiteshvara.

The misery of jealousy,
The strife and quarrels of the demi-gods,
May the cause and effect of this suffering be absorbed into me.
The patience of my three doors
And all virtuous roots of non-jealousy
I give to all beings who are equal to space.
By emptying the realm of quarreling demi-gods,
May they attain the sublime all-accomplishing wisdom,
The Karma family of Avalokiteshvara.

All who are overcome by the mind of arrogance,
The gods who experience death and downfall,
May the cause and effect of this suffering be absorbed into me.
Pure, diligent undertaking
And all the virtuous roots of non-pride
I give to beings who are equal to space.
By emptying the realm of dying and falling gods,
May they attain the wisdom of equanimity,
The Jewel family of Avalokiteshvara.

Countless karmic obstructions without beginning,
The basis for circling in birth, old age, sickness, and death,
May the cause and effect of this suffering be absorbed into me.
The virtuous roots of my body, speech, and mind
Accumulated from beginningless time
I give to all beings who are as vast as space.
By emptying the realm of speedy and impoverished humans,

May they attain the supreme wisdom of pristine awareness,
The stainless dharmakaya of Avalokiteshvara.

Through the instructions of the vinaya, bodhisattvayana, and
    secret mantrayana,
May faults, downfalls, and broken commitments be absorbed
    into me.
The virtue of maintaining the three precepts
I give to beings who are equal to space.
Having purified the three precepts,
With not a whiff of degradation arising,
May they obtain the embodiment of the Vajrasattva family.

Damaging and destroying the three supports cuts the life force.
May the karmic obscurations for a shortened life be absorbed
    into me.
Upholding the three supports and the virtue of a protected life
I give to all beings who are as vast as space.
With no notion of untimely death,
May they attain Vajra Amitayus.

When the diseases of wind and bile form,
May all the illnesses of beings be absorbed into me.
Abandoning beating and striking, giving medicine and such,
All the roots of virtue of well-being and happiness free from
    disease
I give to all beings who are as vast as space.
May they obtain Bendur, the body of light,
The Medicine Buddha to cure the three illnesses.

Through stealing, not giving and taking,
May hunger, thirst, and destitution be absorbed into me.
All the fruit of generosity and spiritual wealth

I give to beings who are as vast as space.
May all desires effortlessly and spontaneously
Be the enjoyment of sky treasures.

Creating only non-virtue,
Born into impure realms,
May all karmic obscurations be absorbed into me.

The motivation to develop the ten and such
I give to all beings who are as vast as space.
Into the pure realms of True Joy and Great Bliss,
May they be born.

By meditating solely with wrong views,
Not delighted by the rare and sublime,
May all these karmic obscurations be absorbed into me.
The roots of virtue from the three types of faith
I give to all beings who are as vast as space.
With confidence in the results of infallible karma
Bursting from the heart,
May it produce the cultivation of virtue and the avoidance of
    wrongdoing.
Through familiarization with ego-clinging alone,
Seeing the enemy of self-projections,
May attachment and aversion be absorbed into me.

The virtuous roots of the four immeasurables
I give to all beings who are as vast as space.
May they have thoughts of love and compassion,
Joy and equanimity.

The mind that holds deluded perceptions as real,
May this source of suffering be absorbed into me.

The realization of the empty ground of egolessness
I give to all beings who are as vast as space.
By giving rise to the experience of profound emptiness,
May they attain the supreme state of complete enlightenment.

The sixteen fears and such,
The inability to meet with relatives,
Or find a place with food, wealth, and friends,
Separation from one's wishes,
The task of subduing enemies and protecting relatives,
The inability to maintain possession
Of power, riches, and reputation,
Never finding what is sought,
Sudden obstacles, instinctive fears and the like,
For these sufferings of change,
I take on all ego-clinging.

All genuine merit of the three times,
Good fortune, authentic presence, and vital body
I give without interruption to all beings
So that all sentient beings have joy and comfort,
And enter into the experience of enlightenment.

To those who have requested the propitious dharma teachings,
Who have given food to eat, yogurt to drink, and animals to ride,
All food, riches, and veneration provided to me,
To those who take pleasure in wrong views and lack faith,
Who rob, beat, and hit with malicious intent toward me,
Linked by positive and negative karma,
Just as they see me,
Recalling my faults and qualities when they hear my name,
And all beings who are aware of me,
By removing beginningless obstacles and negativities,

Through the great compassion of the exalted ones,
May they be guided to Dewachen.

By the actions of my three doors,
Including the smell of my body,
May I be able to benefit beings.
Through harm to my body,
By the ill will of humans and non-humans,
May they immediately attain enlightenment.
If even slightly because of me,
May the fruit of wrongdoing never be accumulated.

Like a dream, the reflection of the moon on water, or a mirage,
In examining the lack of true existence,
This ego-clinging has deceived everyone.
I and all beings equal to space,
The obstructing spirits, non-humans and the like
Are equal in the emptiness of the absolute.
May all mother and father sentient beings
Not be deceived by clinging to what is empty as real.

In the relative all beings have been our mothers and fathers.
With respect to the parents of the world
And all their great kindness,
It is a mistake to carry malice between mother and child.
Therefore consider all mother and father sentient beings
With impartiality and remember their kindness.

Give victory and gain to others,
Take defeat and loss upon oneself.
By the strength of this highest intention,
Having perfected accumulations and purified obscurations,
Precious supreme bodhicitta,

Emptiness suffused with compassion,
The incontrovertible path of the Victorious One,
Having quickly and easily taken birth,
May we swiftly obtain omniscient buddhahood.

From one with virtuous aspirations and determination to practice mind training, Lodro Thaye has written these words from the solitude of a mountain hermitage.

Root Verses of the Seven Points of Mind Training

I. The Preliminaries Teach the Foundation of Dharma Practice
   1. First, train in the preliminaries.

II. The Main Practice: Training in Bodhicitta
   Absolute Bodhicitta: Attendant Meditation
   2. Consider all phenomena as a dream.
   3. Examine the nature of unborn awareness.
   4. The antidote in itself is liberated.
   5. Rest in the nature of the alaya.
   6. In post-meditation, be a child of illusion.
   Relative Bodhicitta: Principal Meditation
   7. Practice giving and taking alternately. Mount both upon the breath.
   8. Three objects, three poisons, and three roots of virtue.
   9. In all conduct train with maxims.
   10. Begin the sequence of taking with oneself.

III. Transforming Adversity into the Path of Enlightenment
   11. When the world is full of evil, transform misfortune into the path of awakening.

Relative Bodhicitta
12. Realize all faults spring from one source.
13. Meditate upon gratitude toward all.
Absolute Bodhicitta
14. Meditate upon illusory appearance as the four kayas. This is the unsurpassable protection of emptiness.
Special Practices
15. The four practices are the best of means.
16. Use whatever you face as a practice immediately.

IV. An Explanation of the Practices as a Way of Life
What to Do during This Life
17. The pith instructions briefly summarized: apply the five strengths.
What to Do at the Moment of Death
18. The Mahayana instructions for the transference of consciousness are the five strengths. Conduct is vital.

V. Measures of Proficiency in Mind Training
19. All dharma agrees at a single point.
20. Of the two witnesses, rely on the main one.
21. Always maintain a joyful attitude.
22. You have reached proficiency if you can practice even while distracted.

VI. Commitments of Mind Training
23. Always train in the three basic principles.
24. Transform your attitude and remain natural.
25. Do not speak about the downfalls of others.
26. Do not ponder others' business.
27. Train with the strongest emotions first.
28. Abandon any expectation of fruition.
29. Abstain from toxic food.

30. Do not be a loyalist.
31. Do not be contentious.
32. Do not wait in ambush.
33. Do not pounce upon vulnerability.
34. Do not transfer the dzo's load onto the ox.
35. Do not be competitive.
36. Do not twist the practice.
37. Do not bring a god down to the level of a demon.
38. Do not seek out others' suffering as the limbs of your delight.

VII. Guidelines for Mind Training
39. Use one practice for everything.
40. Use a single corrective for everything.
41. Two things to do: one at the beginning, one at the end.
42. Whichever of the two arises, be patient.
43. Protect the two as dearly as your life.
44. Train in the three difficulties.
45. Take up the three principal causes.
46. Practice to not let the three degenerate.
47. Remain inseparable from the three.
48. Practice impartially toward everything. Deep and comprehensive mastery overall is essential.
49. Always meditate on whatever is most challenging.
50. Do not rely on other factors.
51. Practice what is essential now.
52. Do not dwell in misunderstanding.
53. Do not be sporadic.
54. Train wholeheartedly.
55. Find liberation through both reflection and analysis.
56. Do not feel the world owes you.
57. Do not be reactive.
58. Do not be temperamental.
59. Do not self-aggrandize.

Mangala Shri Bhuti

Mangala Shri Bhuti (MSB) is a nonprofit Tibetan Buddhist organization under the direction of Venerable Dzigar Kongtrul Rinpoche. MSB has centers in Colorado, Vermont, Ireland, Brazil, and Japan, which offer programs on introductory and advanced Buddhist topics. Elizabeth Mattis Namgyel (author of *The Power of an Open Question*) and Dungse Jampal Norbu also teach widely under the umbrella of MSB.

Every Sunday, at noon Eastern Standard Time, MSB broadcasts the "Link," a live teaching by Rinpoche or one of his students. MSB also offers online courses led by senior students that introduce key principles of Hinayana, Mahayana, and Vajrayana Buddhism, and provide information for those interested in deepening their studies with Dzigar Kongtrul Rinpoche. To learn about any of these teachings and to find out more about Rinpoche and his community, please visit www.mangalashribhuti.org.

If you would like to listen to recordings of Rinpoche's teachings, visit our MSB Store, www.msbstore.org. Finally, MSB is building the Sangdo Palri Temple of Wisdom and Compassion in Crestone, Colorado. This temple for world peace and spiritual awakening will be complete in 2017. For more information, go to msbsangdopalri.org.